Heaven Couldn't Wait.

A Gospel for the powerless,
in a world of performance.

Phelim Doherty

WESTBOW
PRESS®
A DIVISION OF THOMAS NELSON
& ZONDERVAN

Copyright © 2026 Phelim Doherty.

All rights reserved. No part of this book may be used or reproduced by any means, graphic, electronic, or mechanical, including photocopying, recording, taping or by any information storage retrieval system without the written permission of the author except in the case of brief quotations embodied in critical articles and reviews.

This book is a work of non-fiction. Unless otherwise noted, the author and the publisher make no explicit guarantees as to the accuracy of the information contained in this book and in some cases, names of people and places have been altered to protect their privacy.

WestBow Press books may be ordered through booksellers or by contacting:

WestBow Press
A Division of Thomas Nelson & Zondervan
1151 W. 2nd St
Bloomington, IN 47403
www.westbowpress.com
844-714-3454

Because of the dynamic nature of the Internet, any web addresses or links contained in this book may have changed since publication and may no longer be valid. The views expressed in this work are solely those of the author and do not necessarily reflect the views of the publisher, and the publisher hereby disclaims any responsibility for them.

Any people depicted in stock imagery provided by Getty Images are models, and such images are being used for illustrative purposes only. Certain stock imagery © Getty Images.

ISBN: 979-8-3850-6667-4 (sc)
ISBN: 979-8-3850-6668-1 (e)

Print information available on the last page.

WestBow Press rev. date: 12/22/2025

Scripture quotations are taken from the Holy Bible, NEW INTERNATIONAL VERSION®, NIV® Copyright © 1973, 1978, 1984, 2011 by Biblica, Inc.® Used by permission. All rights reserved worldwide.

Scripture quotations are taken from the Holy Bible, New Living Translation, copyright © 1996, 2004, 2015 by Tyndale House Foundation. Used by permission of Tyndale House Publishers Inc., Carol Stream, Illinois 60188. All rights reserved.

Scripture quotations are taken from the NEW AMERICAN STANDARD BIBLE®, Copyright © 1960, 1962, 1963, 1968, 1971, 1972, 1973, 1975, 1977, 1995 by The Lockman Foundation. Used by permission.

Scripture quotations are from the Good News Translation in Today's English Version- Second Edition Copyright © 1992 by American Bible Society. Used by Permission.

The Holy Bible, Berean Standard Bible, BSB. Copyright ©2016, 2020 by Bible Hub. Used by Permission. All Rights Reserved Worldwide.

Scripture quotations are taken from the New King James Version. Copyright © 1982 by Thomas Nelson, Inc. Used by permission. All rights reserved.

Scripture quotations are taken from THE MESSAGE, copyright © 1993, 2002, 2018 by Eugene H. Peterson. Used by permission of NavPress. All rights reserved. Represented by Tyndale House Publishers, Inc.

The Holy Bible, Berean Standard Bible, BSB. Copyright ©2016, 2020 by Bible Hub. Used by Permission. All Rights Reserved Worldwide.

Contents

Dedication ix
Foreword xi
Introduction xv

1 Heaven couldn't wait. That's news, not advice. 1
2 A gospel for the powerless, not a religion for the pious. . . . 11
3 Church begotten, not made. From eternal
    students to eternal sons. 22
4 The Father who never left us to save ourselves. 31
5 Brighter than the Sun: The Extravagance of God. 40
6 When the Gospel dawns: Repentance toward God. 48
7 A presentation of power. The Gospel and the Spirit. 58
8 Perplexed by the Gospel. 71
9 Honey, we shrunk the Gospel!. 82
10 The authority of intimacy: Living from union
    in a world of separation. 90
11 The Life of Obedience; His. 100
12 Heavenly Government: the empowerment to be. 114
13 The Dawn that death flees from. 124

Epilogue 135

Dedication

To my parents,
Patrick and Noreen.

'A marriage made in heaven'.

Foreword

Barely a fortnight after re-reading the C. S. Lewis classic, *Mere Christianity*, I have now had the joy of reading Phelim Doherty's latest manuscript, *Heaven Couldn't Wait*. Very different works, obviously. But for sheer depth of insight and burden-lifting, soul-refreshing, undeniable biblical truth, I find myself even more uplifted by my friend than by that other fine Irishman.

Now, only weeks after Phelim so willingly and effortlessly penned the foreword for my own latest offering, I find myself with a much harder return task. While Phelim graciously plucked out some pithy quotes from my draft to whet the reader's appetite, were I to attempt the same, there's barely a paragraph I couldn't draw from. Page by page, this is a heavyweight masterpiece that, even in the smallest of doses, defies the gravitational pull of earth-bound religion and philosophy intent on sucking us down from the heights to which, as believers, we have already been raised by the Gospel.

Like Phelim's earlier work, *The Father We Never Knew*, everyone needs to read this book. As you read it yourself, I challenge you to tell me of any person you know, from Christian to atheist, who would not benefit wonderfully from the infusion of its life-transforming light.

If this book is read as it was written, it will set hearers free from taskmasters of religious performance and self-improvement, and open up a world where the grace, presence and power of a God whom we could never reach, have already reached down to us in

Jesus, a world where we no longer need to prove ourselves, but live out of the love and joy of the One who first loved us.

Phelim and I are 'Celtic cousins' with a similar Gaelic heritage, his Donegal Irish and mine Scottish Hebridean. Though we grew up barely 200 miles apart we lived in a different religious universe, his Catholic and ritualistic and mine Calvinist and austere. But were we really poles apart? Listening to Phelim, I've discovered that our experiences were remarkably similar.

I smile in a way you can only with lengthy hindsight, as I remember the otherwise sunny Sabbath Day our family squeezed into one of many then-packed-now-empty church buildings. As my siblings and I giggled in the rear pews, the grave-faced Presbyterian minister suddenly paused from his wooden turret, eyeballed us over his half-rimmed spectacles, and stopped everyone's breath with the sombre, humiliating rebuke, *"This is no laughing matter."*

"No Laughing Matter" could be an apt epithet for Phelim's and my early experiences of church. The irony is that our Protestant and Catholic instructors, though commanding us in opposite theological directions, brought us to exactly the same place.

As Phelim puts it so simply and beautifully, *"Every religion says 'Do!' The gospel declares, 'Done!'"* The pretend gods that man creates after his own image, in common with atheism and a world of self-help philosophy, drown us with good advice. But the gospel is not good advice, Phelim reminds us. It is good news. The gospel delivers us from the whip of *Do-this-and-God-might*, and into the provision of *He-did-so-you-have*. Salvation, joy, peace, the loving embrace of God Himself, are received – not achieved – by, and only by, grace through faith. The gospel offers us the present experience of eternal life, as we not only believe in Him but come to know Him through the most wonderful gift of grace ever bestowed: the Person of the Holy Spirit, God Himself.

But before you read, just one last thing about Phelim. He likes to write his sermons. If you are like me, little does more to deflate the lungs than the prospect of a well-written sermon! Unless it's

Phelim. He is among the best platform communicators out there, but his pen is just as anointed as his lips. And as I read Phelim's labour of love, I realise his gems were inspired in print before ever heard through a microphone. To all those who prefer the paperback to the movie, I say the same: the preacher's great, but you absolutely must read the book.

Alistair Matheson
Senior Minister, Glasgow City Church.

Introduction

> *"Now we have received, not the spirit of the world, but the Spirit who is from God, that we might know the things that have been freely given to us by God."*
> 1 Corinthians 2:12.[1]

This is not a self-help book. It is not written to motivate you to somehow do better for God. Rather, it is an attempt to express the inexpressible, the extravagance of a God who so loves us that He has embraced our life and our death.

The best gods this world can imagine are ones who remain in their heaven waiting for men to work their way there by the strength of their own piety. But in Jesus Christ we saw a god not leaving us to save ourselves, but one descending into the depths of our separation, that He might carry us to the heights of His union. He is the God who went down with our ship so that we could be raised in His, the fellowship of the Father and Son in the Spirit. Here is a love brighter than the sun, a dawn that even death pales before, and one that our natural minds cannot bear.

Jesus knew that no man could comprehend such a love and so promised His disciples that after He had departed, the Father would send another like Him, light from light, to lead us into the truth (John 14:16, 16:12, 13)[2]. The Holy Spirit had to come, because it is

---

[1] New King James Version.
[2] New King James Version.

only the presence of the dawn, not the promise of it, that makes the darkness flee. How are men to know the depths of their darkness if they have never seen light? So too the love of God cannot be believed without being experienced, and so the proclamation of the Gospel in the power of the Spirit is not an exercise in mere motivation but an experience of translation. It is to find yourself in the presence of God, with the darkness of unbelief receding and the kingdom of the Son dawning on you. It is to find your heart persuaded of what is, not what might be, and most startling of all, it is to find that His desire was never to make heaven our home one day, but us His home today. Heaven couldn't wait!

We need this wind from heaven because we have been brought up in a world of a different spirit. A world that does not know a saviour has only ever taught us to be our own. The spirit of this world cannot speak to us of what has been freely given. It is man-centred and so can only speak of us as the primary agent of our own salvation. In a world that revolves around us, God is reduced to a size that will fit our transactional mindset. He becomes a god made in our image, a god we can do business with. If we do this for Him, then He will do that for us.

But He is a god that must not be reduced to one that men can manage, lest they set up their counting tables and call it His temple. He can no more be managed than we can control the wind, and everywhere His Spirit moves, the enormity of what He has freely given begins to dawn. He gives life with a father, not a manager, for there is no higher life to live than that of one who believes God to be their father. With such a father, it is not our repentance that makes His generosity extravagant. It is the revelation of His extravagant generosity that causes us to repent, to find our beliefs utterly changed, and our hearts at rest in the storms of this world. Any earthly orator can preach up a storm that stirs the flesh to action, but only the gospel of heaven still causes men to wonder that even the wind and waves in their own heart obey and are still.

'Here is what you need to do to save yourself' sounds like

great advice, but the effect of believing that I am the author of my salvation is to fall. We fall from living in the wide-open spaces of God's extravagance to the small prison cell that is a life consumed with saving itself. But as Paul and Silas discovered, even prison cells can be filled with heaven by an extravagant God! (Acts 16:23-26).

Whatever the dark situation of your life right now, which appears to have you imprisoned in a confined place, I pray that this book will cause you to look up and behold Christ, and by His Spirit, find your heart persuaded that He is who He claimed to be, your God and your Saviour. In receiving Him, you will find that all of heaven is crammed into your cell. In that cell with you is a God so extravagant, so unreasonably gracious, that He has made His home in your pit of darkness, and even the night will now shine like the day (Psalm 139:7-12). In that hour you will know that only a love that is not measured out to you according to your behaviour, is powerful enough to change your behaviour. I have found that a god who only gives to me according to what I first give to Him, is too much like me to save me!

So don't give me a god who is just another counter of my sins against me. Let me have the one who turned over the tables of the counters! Let me have Emmanuel, God with us, for I find that He is like the dawn. Like the sun rising, it is not the promise of Him but the presence of Him that drives the darkness out of my life. I find that the gospel that brings His presence is not mere instruction on what might be, but the news of what now is. To proclaim the gospel on earth as it is in heaven is not to declare what might be if you. It is to declare what is, because Christ! The song of heaven is not "One day, if you." It is "Today, because He! The Gospel is the revelation that *"Behold, now is the accepted time; behold, now is the day of salvation."*[3] (2 Corinthians 6:1,2)

This is what it is to preach Christ, but unfortunately, I find myself living in a world that has only ever preached me! Such a

---

[3] New King James Version.

world has so conformed my thoughts to the earthly realm that I have only ever looked to myself to produce a good life. In the light of His glory and grace, the light of His presence, I can now see that I was so consumed with being right by myself, I couldn't hear the Gospel as good news. My self-dependency could only ever hear it as good advice. Let me say that differently. I was too religious to take in what God was saying to me. My hope was so much in my behaviour, that it was only when all hope in myself was exhausted that I finally began to look higher than myself for life.

The god of religion promises to meet you at your best one day in heaven. But the God of all grace meets with us in the pigpen. It is there, when we finally realise that we are powerless to be as He is, apart from Him, that we can bow our heads and say what Mary did, *"May it be done to me according to your Word"*[4] (Luke 1:38). Mary was never asked to produce a life *for* God but to partake of the life *of* God, that she might bear His life. The Gospel is the impartation of the life of God, and all who are thirsty, all who will receive this living water, will find Jesus' words to be true. His life, eternal life, springs up like a fountain within them (John 4:14).

This was never a story about me but always one about us. The person I grew up to be was formed by the family whose life I shared, and you will read in these pages that I was blessed to be raised in a loving family. But family was always the creation of He who was a Father before He was a creator. His love has always desired that each of us would be raised at His table, raised in the fellowship of the Father and the Son, having been begotten of His Spirit through the gospel (1 Corinthians 4:15). This world has only offered us endless instruction, when all we ever needed was to know our eternal father, for knowing Him and the life He has given is eternal life (John 17:3). We were not made by ourselves or for ourselves, but for Him who knew us before our earthly family ever did (Jeremiah 1:5).

When I look to Christ, I find that my life is at peace with God

---

[4] New American Standard Bible.

and men, for I stop trying to save myself. But when I listen to the wind and the waves of this world, the voices of earthly-minded men and women, I find my gaze falling from Christ and my peace being stolen. Suddenly I am fighting my corner, grasping to make a better life for myself, and taking offence at those who are not helping me to save myself. In those moments, like Peter sinking below the waves of that storm, I need to feel the strong grip of Jesus take hold of me to hold me up. This is what I experience when I sit under the gospel of God's grace, as opposed to the worldly gospel of my piety. I feel the strength of His life upholding me, His everlasting arms beneath me.

When men try and reason out salvation apart from the Spirit of God, religion (self-effort) is always the result. This is because religion to the natural, earthly man appears the only reasonable way by which he can obtain the blessings of God. Multitudes of us have been blinded by a reasonable gospel. The only gospel with the power to open our eyes to the truth is the one that sounds like foolishness to the reasonable man: Christ and Him crucified (1 Corinthians 2:1-5). It is not a religion for the pious; it is a gospel for the powerless in a world of performance.

Throughout these pages you will find certain phrases appear again and again. To quote the apostle Paul, *"I don't mind repeating what I have written before, and you will be safer if I do so."*[5] (Philippians 3:1). He who has ears, let him hear. Heaven couldn't wait!

Phelim Doherty

---

[5] Good News Translation.

Chapter One

Heaven couldn't wait.
That's news, not advice.

. . . .

Monday, 2 January 2023, was a beautiful day. After days of rain, the sky cleared, and the sun shone on the little church in which my mother's funeral mass was taking place and on the ground in which she would be buried. She had just passed her eighty-eighth birthday and died the week after Christmas, surrounded by her seven children and my father. He had been with her almost every day of the last ten years of her decline with dementia. Although she had no idea what time of year it was, she had somehow managed one last time to gather her children around her for Christmas. She had always worked so hard each Christmas to make those occasions such a celebration of our family life, and they remain my most vivid childhood memories.

I was given the privilege of speaking at her funeral, and so I shared my conviction that Mum was now sitting with her Saviour, not sad or confused anymore but at a great feast full of joy and laughter and wonder, a celebration over her. I said that I believed this because I believed Jesus to be full of joy, laughter, and love, and that one evidence of this was the name His religious opponents came to call Him by. They said of Him, "Here is a glutton and a drunkard, a friend of tax collectors and sinners" (Matthew 11:19).[6] Why would the religious call Him that? Because when you went looking for Jesus, you would invariably find Him speaking not from a platform but from a table.

I believe He loved the way a table brought everyone to the same level because everyone must eat, and it was for this purpose that He came: so that He could enter the fellowship of our humanity, and we could share in the fellowship of His Father. He would have loved the communion of life that uniquely takes place at a table, where families gather to have the most basic need of our humanity met and share what they have with one another.

Now you might think, *So what? If He was always at a table, I can see how that might give observers the impression He was a glutton, that He liked to eat, but what made those watching Him from a distance think that He drank a lot at those tables?* If you walked into a restaurant full of diners at various tables and were asked to immediately choose which table you thought the most wine was being consumed at, how would you choose? I would simply listen for the laughter. I believe they thought Jesus was a drunkard because of the joy emanating from His table!

I remember the morning when I first heard people dare to laugh in church. I was a teenager attending mass, and the priest told a funny story as an illustration for his sermon. I don't remember what his subject was, but I do remember the shock I felt at the reaction of the people present. It was the first time I ever heard a congregation laugh in a church. Admittedly it was a bit of a nervous laugh. I think I wasn't the only one who suspected the priest was now about to be struck dead on the spot for making us laugh in such a holy place!

Back then, growing up in the church, many of us had the distinct impression that religion was not something to be enjoyed as much as endured. Of all the religious images and pictures we had, not one of

---

[6] New international Version.

them ever showed our Lord or any of the saints laughing. Religion was a serious business, as apparently God never laughed. Yet the gospels tell us that so many parents kept bringing their children to Jesus that His disciples began to rebuke them to keep them from Him. As He entered Jerusalem on Palm Sunday, it was the exuberant joy of the children in a "holy" place that offended the Pharisees (Matthew 21:15–16). As He bent down to pick up children, I can only see a look of joy on Jesus's face.

As far as heaven is concerned, the good news of the gospel and joy cannot be separated. Listen again to the first words of the angel to the shepherds on the night of Jesus's birth: "Do not be afraid; for behold, I bring you good news of great joy which will be for all the people" (Luke 2:10).[7] According to this heavenly messenger, the news about Jesus should bring "mega" joy to all people. Notice the angel never said that he brought good instruction of great joy, but good news. There is a joy in hearing news that no amount of advice can match. Thus, in each generation, how much we have diluted news with instruction can be gauged by the level of joy our "news" elicits. Now think of how many people you know today who, on seeing a sign saying, "Gospel Meeting," would immediately think of the defining mark of such a gathering as "great joy"! In truth, even a little joy is not on most people's radar when they hear the phrase "the gospel". Did the angel get it wrong, or are we missing something about "the gospel"? Why do so many of us now associate that phrase with a message about what we need to do for God, to "get right" with Him? Would it surprise you to hear that such a description is almost the opposite of what the gospel is?

The word translated as "gospel" in the New Testament is the Greek word *euangelion*.[8] It literally means "the good announcement",

---

[7] New American Standard Bible.
[8] Strongs Number 2098. https://www.blueletterbible.org/lexicon/g2098/kjv/tr/0-1/

and it most often referred to the announcement made to a city or a nation of what rule or kingdom they were now under. In ancient times whole cities would wait with bated breath for a messenger to bring word of the outcome of a battle. That news, of either victory or defeat, would spell life or death for that city. Imagine then the joy of those people when the messenger with the euangelion, the good announcement, the "gospel", arrived. It was the news that they had been delivered from death. No messenger in the ancient world arriving at a city with the euangelion ever brought advice; he brought news!

This explains why the record of the early church in the book of Acts is full of accounts of revivals and riots. There was either great rejoicing over or violent reaction to the gospel that the apostles preached. Whole cities do not turn out to hear advice but to hear news (Acts 13:44)! This good announcement caused such a stir across the Roman Empire that those who proclaimed it were accused of having "turned the world upside down" (Acts 17:6).[9] All this brings me to a question. What happened? What happened to the gospel?

What has happened to a message that two thousand years ago attracted the bar crowd and repelled the religious but now appears to do exactly the opposite? How did a supernatural message about God's love for us become reduced to one about our love for Him? Where has the joy gone from a message that once went viral across the ancient world, empowering people to love their enemies, but now appears largely confined to church buildings full of folk who often feel we barely have enough love for our neighbours, never mind our enemies! For many years I could not understand why the apostle Paul could describe the gospel as "the power of God" (Romans 1:16),[10] for my experience of church was not of power but of ritual and tradition. Where was this transforming joy that the

---

[9] New King James Version.
[10] New International Version.

gospel brought to the early church, this power to turn nations upside down (Acts 17:6)?

In recent years, by the grace of God, I have come to increasingly understand that the power started to drain from the message as soon as we started adding to it! Each little "helpful" addition in effect subtracted from the announcement, reducing it from one about His love for us to one about our love for Him (1 John 4:10). This wasn't an abrupt change; it happened as slowly as yeast works its way through a loaf (Galatians 5:9). It was death by a thousand cuts (Galatians 5:2–4). Each time men added another little instruction, thinking they were helping people to either "get" saved or "stay" saved, they moved the foundation of our lives from Christ to self (1 Corinthians 3:11; Colossians 3:3–4), and each time we reduced Him, we elevated ourselves to the role of our own Saviour. In this way the message was conformed to our world, for a world that does not know a Saviour can only teach you to be your own, can only ever point you ... to you!

This watering down of the announcement, from one about *His* life for us to one about *our* lives for Him, reduced good news to good advice. Now the good news of "what *is* because He ...", began to sound more like "what *might* be if you ..."! A message that had once left our faith in Christ and His finished work now seemed to be pointing to me and my unfinished life. Why is that such a significant change? Because there is no power in any message that points you to yourself. To proclaim the gospel in the power of God's Spirit is to announce what *is* because He lives, not what might be if only you live holy enough for long enough!

The good news gospel announced that because of what God had done, we could now have Christ as our life (1 Corinthians 1:30), for God Himself had done what we could never do: qualified us to share in His life (Colossians 1:12). But the good advice "gospel" (Galatians 1:6) speaks of His life (eternal life) as something we can only know in the future if we ... Slowly the good news that God had made a way for His presence to be with us today was becoming the good advice on how we could get to God's presence one day. Can you see it yet? A message about knowing Him *today* was being reduced to a message about getting to heaven *one day*. Jesus never taught us to pray about getting to heaven one day but to pray today, *"Your Kingdom come, your will be done on earth as it is in heaven."*[11] (Matthew 6:10)

Which is greater, you getting to heaven or the one who made heaven living in you? Do you know that we have a Father who loves us so much that He could no more wait around for us to somehow find our way to heaven than you could stand back and watch a lost child of yours struggle to make it home and not run and kiss them and wrap them in your arms? In fact, the same word Jesus used to describe the father of the prodigal son *falling* on his son to kiss him (Luke 15:20) is the same one used to describe how the Holy Spirit *fell* on people as they listened to the apostle Peter preach the gospel (Luke 10:44). The truth is that heaven couldn't wait. That's news, not advice!

That's why the New Testament doesn't speak of Christ in heaven one day as our hope, but Christ in us *today* (Colossians 1:27). When the apostle Paul described the gospel as *"the power of God unto salvation"*[12] (Romans 1:16), he wasn't talking about getting to heaven one day, but the power that comes from receiving the presence of God today—the power to live unafraid of death (Hebrews 2:14, 15). This power is His Spirit in us, persuading us that we are a child of God and now share in His life, a life that has overcome sin and death (Romans 8:16, John 16:33).

Do you know that every time someone defers your hope to some day in the future, they sicken your heart? The Bible says, *"Hope deferred makes the heart sick."*[13] What is the antidote to such a sick heart, a heart powerless to transform itself? Listen to the rest of that

---

[11] New King James Version.
[12] King James Bible.
[13] New Living Translation.

verse: *"Hope deferred makes the heart sick, but a dream fulfilled is a tree of life."*[14] (Proverbs 13:12). Advice is about what might be, but news is about what is. The Gospel is good news, not good advice! It is a dream fulfilled, a tree of life. It is life-giving, not life-taking.

That's why the Bible never records God's Spirit speaking to a person of who they *could* be, but only of who they *are* (Genesis 17:5, Judges 6:12, Acts 9:13-15, Romans 8:16). The call of this world on your life is to *become* someone by what you do, but God doesn't call us to become someone by our own strength. He calls us to *be* whom He declares us to be by His grace (1 Corinthians 15:10). In fact, it is only by the power of God's Spirit in a person that they can even live as who God declares them to be (John 15:5, Luke 24:49). The wonderful news of the Gospel is that God so loves people that through the gift of His Son and His Spirit, whoever wants to know God as their father and share in the eternal life of His Son now can (John 3:16). That's because this announcement, this gospel, carries the power to deliver people from the darkness of unbelief into the light of knowing Him, for to see Jesus dying for you is to see how much your father in heaven truly loves you (John 14:9). When you know how much God is for you, you will never have to live in this life as a victim, no matter what this world has taken from you (Romans 8:31, 32). That's because knowing Him is to see that all the rejection in the world can't hold a candle to the acceptance you have in Christ! (2 Corinthians 4:17).

It is by the light of this gospel of good news that men can see we have a father who never left us to save ourselves, for Jesus' life, death, resurrection, ascension, and abiding intercession *is* God not leaving us to save ourselves. This news, this gospel of heaven that leaves our faith in Christ, is so far above the religion of earth (that always leaves our faith in ourselves) that we cannot even believe it apart from the presence of God's Spirit (1 Corinthians 12:3). What a good father. He never even left us to believe by ourselves!

---

[14] New Living Translation.

This is what Jesus meant when He said, *"Apart from me, you can do nothing."*[15] (John 15:5).

I know this sounds too good to be true, but our Father in heaven's love for us is not a love that is merely transactional: if you do this for me, then I will do that for you. You might have spent a lifetime promising God how good you will be one day, thinking that then He will be good to you, but you are two thousand years too late. When Jesus stretched out his arms on that cross, that *was* the Father embracing you and I in all our sin and burying us in Himself, just as Jesus described the father of the prodigal running towards his son and burying him in a bear hug (Luke 15:20). If you remember Jesus' story, that son had a plan to save himself (Luke 15:18, 19). In effect he had said to himself, 'I will show my father how sorry I am by working for him as a slave, so that he will save me from death.' But as soon as the father heard that his son was planning to try and save himself by working harder, he knew that his son needed to know right then and there that everything the father had was already his (Luke 15:22, 23). How desperately so many of us in the church need to know the same, that salvation is not of ourselves but is the gift of God (Ephesians 2:8, 9).

The Father's response to His son's need is to immediately dress him as a son of His should be dressed. He is given the best cloak, ring, and shoes, and a celebration is commanded. It is crucial that we realise that the Father did not do this to convince Himself that this beggar before him is His son, but to convince the son! Contrary to what earthly religion teaches men, God does not have to be convinced of who we are by the outward appearance of our lives. In fact, our outward lives only reveal what *we* are convinced of (Luke 6:45). The life you are leading is the one you are believing in! (Proverbs 4:23). Our actions are only the branches of our life. The root is what our hearts are believing. Jesus didn't come to take an axe to the branches but to the root (Ezekiel 36:26).

---

[15] New American Standard Bible.

The Bible uses a Greek word to describe this transformation in what our hearts are believing: 'metanoia.'[16] We are more familiar with our English translation of that word, 'repentance,' but unfortunately the way the word 'repent' is now commonly used does a disservice to the original meaning. The Gospel is not about mere behaviour modification but a total transformation of the root of a person's life—what they are believing (John 6:28, 29). Any change in behaviour must be the fruit of a change of heart, and this profound change of heart only comes by an encounter with the love of God, His true nature, His Spirit (Romans 5:5).

When men water down the gospel to "Change your behaviour and God will give Himself to you," they are presenting a god made in our image, a self-centred god. Any love that is measured to me according to my behaviour, is not powerful enough to change my behaviour. A god who only gives to me according to what I first give to Him is too much like me to save me. Don't give me a god who is just another counter of my sins against me. Let me have the one who turned over the tables of the counters! (Matthew 21:12, 2 Corinthians 5:19) It is not our repentance that makes God's generosity extravagant. It is the revelation of His extravagant generosity that causes us to repent, to find our beliefs utterly changed, and the extravagant thirst of our hearts quenched (Romans 2:4). Only a love that is greater than my death can undo my death (Romans 8:38, 39).

Jesus saw the religious leaders placing heavy burdens of required behaviour on people, and He called those leaders hypocrites and *'white-washed tombs'*[17] (Matthew 23:27, 28), for He knew that there had been no inner transformation of the heart underneath all that religious posturing. No matter how respectable the outer life may appear to men's eyes, God sees the fear and lust that moves the heart of each of us to try and save ourselves by our own works. When asked what work God requires of us, Jesus' answer was simple. *"This

---

[16] Strongs Number G3340.
[17] New International Version.

is the work of God, that you believe in Him whom He has sent."[18] (John 6:29). This is the revelation of God in Christ that undoes the lie that God withheld Himself from us. He is the God who so loves us that He gave all that He had to give, not after we had reached some standard of self-effort, but while we were powerless. (Romans 5:6). This is a gospel for the powerless, not a religion for the pious!

You see, apart from God's extravagant Spirit, our earthly minds are too frugal and miserly to think or imagine a god so loving that His way of loving us is not to stand back from us but to fall on our dirty lives and embrace us into Himself. He embraced our lonely life and our lonely death. He is the God who went down with our ship so that the way could be made for us to rise up in His; the fellow ship of the Father and the Son, in the Spirit (John 17:21-23). You see, heaven couldn't wait. That is news, not advice!

---

[18] New American Standard Bible.

Chapter Two

A gospel for the powerless, not a religion for the pious.

· · · ·

My father qualified as a veterinary surgeon in Dublin in 1957. He came top of his class and could have taken up a nine-to-five job with a government department and a secure future. But he had a passion for veterinary medicine and so plunged straight into the hectic and physically challenging world of farm animal practice. Inspired by his passion, I followed in his footsteps exactly 30 years later. It took me some years to discover that a passion to be like my father was never going to be enough to sustain me through the challenges of that profession. It was only in recent years (while listening to a seminar on health and safety on farms) that it struck me why I had never encouraged any of my children to follow in my footsteps. The job was simply too dangerous, especially at the breakneck speed I had been attempting it. Doctors don't tend to get kicked, bitten, crushed, or gored by their patients, and when you add driving half-asleep at night down lonely country roads, it wasn't a recipe for a long life!

One day in the early 1970s, my father went to visit his local GP, whom he knew well. It wasn't a social visit. His family was concerned about the increasing and unrelenting schedule of work he was facing each week. Being in single-handed practice in those days meant he was mostly on call continually, and his sleep was frequently disrupted by emergency calls. His doctor could find nothing wrong with him physically. After asking him to recount a typical week and hearing of the sheer volume of work he was getting through, his doctor asked him one last question: "Do you enjoy your work?" My father did not need to consider his answer. He readily confessed to loving the job he was doing. His doctor smiled and said to him, "Then don't worry, for you are much healthier than the guy sitting in an office every day watching the clock and dying for 5pm to arrive." That doctor is long gone, but Dad turned 93 last month and continues to inspire all his children. What looked to so many as a lifestyle that was life-taking was, in fact, for my father, life-giving!

Have you ever held an opinion that you later discovered to be the opposite of the truth? Such opinions don't matter if they concern incidental things, but what if my understanding of the most fundamental truth of life is wrong? What if I believe that God is always requiring me to produce something for Him, when in truth He is the life-giver, not the life-taker?

What do you see if I ask you to imagine Christ now looking directly at you? Luke's gospel tells us that as Peter was disowning Jesus for the third time, the rooster crowed, and Jesus looked straight at him. At that moment Peter remembered Jesus' words, *"Before the rooster crows today, you will disown me three times,"*[19] and he burst into tears (Luke 22:61). But how could the look on Jesus' face have been one of disappointment or anger when He already knew how weak and incapable Peter was? I believe His face was full of compassion, and that is what broke Peter.

Think of a point in your life when you were at your most selfish. How do you picture Christ looking at you in that moment? It is an important question, because scripture tells us that Christ's

---

[19] New International Version.

face, His disposition towards us, is the exact image of His Father. (Colossians 1:15, Hebrews1:3). Whether we know it or not, we all live by the inner picture we carry of 'Our Father who art in Heaven.' For many years, the belief I came away with from church was that our heavenly father was always requiring more of me. I was continually left with the impression that he needed more prayer, more money, more time, more commitment; the list seemed endless! Meanwhile, the strange thing was that my earthly father was only ever looking to give to me, not to take. Even now at 93 years of age, when I bring him out to a café, he will always insist on paying the bill. To his dying day he desires to keep giving to me all he can.

I think the picture of our heavenly Father that many of us grew up with was one where the look on His face towards us was one of disappointment. After all, He had to be disappointed with us all the time, because we were being asked to apologise to Him and plead for His forgiveness all the time! I think it is not difficult to understand why some who grew up in that environment walked away with the distinct impression that Jesus came to save us from the Father rather than from sin and death. That's a serious problem because that mental picture we carry (the belief we hold about God in our hearts) is the very foundation, the root from which our lives grow (Proverbs 4:23).

In Acts 9 we read the account of Saul of Tarsus on his way to persecute Christians in Damascus. Think for a moment of the belief, the picture of the Father that Saul of Tarsus must have had in his heart, to cause him to set out to attack the Church. The god He believed in was not one who loved His enemies! He needed an encounter with Christ for that picture in his heart to change, and what a change that was. He went from hating Christians to loving them because the picture of the Father in his heart (his belief) changed (Acts 9:17-20).

God's way of opening our eyes to the heart of the Father is still the same today; it is through an encounter with Jesus. This is why

Jesus said that *"no one comes to the Father, except through me."*[20] (John 14:6). He was saying, in effect, "If you are believing in a Father who doesn't look like me, one who lays down His life for you, then you are not believing in the Father as He really is. You have not yet come to Him, only your version of Him."

I have good news for many atheists out there. It's quite likely that the version of God that you were presented with and couldn't believe in, Jesus doesn't believe in either! The father that Jesus came to reveal is a friend of tax collectors and sinners, and that includes atheists. This is why the angels at Christ's birth did not declare His incarnation to be good news for just some people, but rather *"good news of great joy which will be for all the people"*[21] (Luke 2:10). The good news is that He loves you so much that He gave all He had to give for you. But it was never His idea that you should be required to believe in Him without knowing Him. How can you trust someone you don't know? If God expected you to just believe in Him without knowing Him, there would be no call for the Holy Spirit (1 Corinthians 12:3). He is the one who is given, *"that we might know the things that have been freely given to us by God"*[22]. (1 Corinthians 2:12)

Jesus said, *"Anyone who has seen me, has seen the Father"*[23] (John 14:9). So, what do we see about the Father when we look at how Jesus was with people who had been burned by religion or broken by rejection? We see Him spending time with them, eating with them, listening to all their questions, and responding to them in a way that convinces them that He is for them, not against them (Luke 7:34). That is what the Holy Spirit has been doing in your life and mine for years, so gently and so patiently, because He doesn't do superficial. He's not looking to chalk you up as a convert but to raise you up as a child of the King. But as we will see later, true love doesn't force its

---

[20] New American Standard Bible.
[21] New American Standard Bible.
[22] New King James Version.
[23] New International Version.

own way on us (1 Corinthians 13:5). The Holy Spirit doesn't remove our free will, but He does come to correct the false picture we may carry of the Father.

For that to happen, each of us needs to see Jesus dying for us and hear in His words the Father say to us, *"For God did not send His Son into the world to condemn the world, but that the world through Him might be saved."*[24] (John 3:17) The Holy Spirit wants us to see the Father as He really is. In other words, He wants us to *know* the Father. When the New Testament speaks of believing in God, it is speaking about more than an intellectual understanding, a head knowledge. Because the Holy Spirit has now been given, the gospel can speak about knowing Him for who He really is—a personal encounter. A personal encounter is an encounter of persons, not merely ideas.

If you had stopped Saul on his way to Damascus and asked him if he believed in God, he would have told you in no uncertain terms that not only did he believe in God, but that his belief in God was zealous and passionate. Unfortunately, a zealous belief in God is the most dangerous type to have when your picture of Him is wrong. It was people who zealously believed in God who crucified Jesus! They believed in God, but they didn't know Him. I have a friend who loves to ask people, "Do you believe in God?" When they answer 'Yes,' he then asks them a second question: "But do you know Him?"

The greatest problem in this world right now isn't the lack of people believing in God. It is that multitudes are claiming to believe in Him but in truth don't know Him at all. Meanwhile, their unChrist-like behaviour is only convincing the rest of the world that they don't want to know Him either!

You see, even unbelievers instinctively know that what you are believing is the root of your behaviour (Proverbs 4:23). If your attitude to people is coldly legalistic—that you look on them and

---

[24] New King James Version.

speak of them as a type rather than a unique person of infinite worth to the Father—then do not be surprised if that person is reluctant to believe in your god. Don't be surprised either that the Holy Spirit rarely shows up to confirm your words!

The New Testament declares Jesus to be the exact representation of the Father's being. As Jesus said to Philip, *"Don't you know me, Philip, even after I have been among you such a long time? Anyone who has seen me has seen the Father. How can you say, 'Show us the Father'?"*[25] (John 14:9) Now look at Jesus openly accepting sinners and sharing His meals with them. Throughout his three years of ministry, we do not see one incident recorded where Jesus refused to eat in the house of someone because of their record. He didn't care if they were a tax collector or a Pharisee, a libertine or a legalist, because He didn't see types. He saw unique and infinitely precious persons, destined to be conformed to the likeness of God through an encounter with Him.

The more Christ-like we become, the less comfortable we should be in seeing or speaking about people as if they are a type. Spiritual maturity is growing into the heart of the Father, the mind of Christ on people, and that means growing up to see people as you would see your own children. No father or mother labels their children into types but rather celebrates the uniqueness and infinite worth of each child. Jesus didn't believe in types. He believed in unique persons, each of infinite worth, and His whole disposition and language toward each individual He met communicated to them their true significance to God (Luke 19:1-5). Let me say that differently. The Pharisees labelled Jesus as *'a friend of tax collectors and sinners.'*[26] (Matthew 11:19). Think about that. The outcasts of religion saw Jesus as their friend. They welcomed Him to their gatherings. Do you know why? Because when Jesus spoke to you, He made you feel as if you were the most important person in the world. That's

---

[25] New International Version.

[26] New International Version.

because to encounter Christ is to encounter the heart of a father for his children, not a manager for his workers.

The infinite worth to the Father of each person is a recurrent theme throughout Jesus' ministry. We see it throughout His parables and in His actions as He repeatedly left the crowds to seek out the one in great need. Jesus said that the whole of heaven rejoices when one person comes to faith (Luke 15:7). Stop for a minute and think of the whole of heaven throwing a party over you. In fact, don't stop for a minute. Take an hour, a day, or a lifetime. You still won't get your head around it! That's how much you are valued in heaven. No wonder Jesus told His disciples to pray that the Father's will be done on the earth as it is in heaven. Imagine what a world we would live in if everyone was valued in that way, if we all felt the same love for the stranger as we do for our own children. This is what a spiritual revival is: people beginning to feel how God feels about people!

Heaven on earth starts with the Church. The Holy Spirit brings a revelation of the Father that both calls and empowers the Church to have a metanoia, to repent in our thinking of people as being only valued by God to the extent that they can earn His forgiveness through their piety. When the Church can't even see her own worth to the Father, then we certainly can't see the worth of the atheist or the stranger (Luke 10:27-37). Such an elder brother Church is quite content to send sinners to work off their debt to God through works of piety. But the Father that Jesus revealed welcomed such people to His table, for He was calling them up to a life lived in His presence, not His absence (Isaiah 55:1, John 7:37). He was calling them according to *His* life for them, not *their* life for Him (2 Peter 1:3). He was calling them according to His purpose and grace eternally given to them, not according to their earthly record (2 Timothy 1:9). The Father that Jesus revealed ran towards the sinner, not from him (Luke 15:20). We bring people a gospel for the powerless, not a religion for the pious!

My place as a Christian was in my father's home as a son. I should never have left that place of rest and been lured away by the spirit of this world (self-effort) that promises that the Father will love me more if only I do more for Him (1 Corinthians 2:12). Christ died that I would live and speak as a son, and to make sure that I could take in the enormity of what that means, He poured out His own Spirit for this purpose: that His Spirit would *"beareth witness with our spirit, that we are the children of God."*[27] (Romans 8:16). This is the work of the Holy Spirit: to convince us that to be redeemed doesn't just mean that our sins are forgiven. It also means that we can live as the apostle John did, amazed at what manner of love it is that would call us the children of God (1 John 3:1). He persuades us that the source of the sin in our lives (our old Adamic nature) has been replaced with the nature of Christ, the last Adam (Galatians 2:20, 2 Peter 1:4). It is *His* life in you that saves you, not your life for Him. It is the life received that saves you, not the life achieved. This is why at the centre of apostolic worship is the breaking of bread (Acts 2:42). The words of the apostle Paul that we quote each Sunday at the communion table are not "What I have *achieved* for the Lord I pass on to you," but rather *"For I received from the Lord what I also passed on to you."*[28] (1 Corinthians 11:23).

By the Holy Spirit we come to know that we do not merely have a 'for' God life; we have a 'from' God life! Jesus never told the woman at the well to produce a life worthy of Him. He promised her that eternal life would spring up in her because of what He was giving her, not demanding from her: "But *whoever drinks the water I give them will never thirst. Indeed, the water I give them will become in them a spring of water welling up to eternal life."*[29] (John 4:14).

Throughout this book we will come back repeatedly to Jesus' parable of the prodigal son, recorded in Luke 15. It is probably the most well-known of all Jesus' parables, and that may be because the revelation it brings, of the true nature of the Father, touches

---

[27] King James Bible.
[28] New International Version.
[29] New International Version.

on our greatest need: to know God (John 17:3). In this parable, the father never wanted his son to live as a servant seeking to earn his forgiveness and love. (Luke 15:21-24) Our heavenly Father also never wanted His love for man to be restrained, held back by being shackled to man's performance. Instead, He found a way to liberate man from the lie that if only he would behave better, then he would be loved better. That way was to give man everything he had. That way was Christ (John 14:6). God held nothing back from us, but not at the time when man had done well, but at the right time, when man had done nothing nor could do anything for Him. *"You see, at just the right time, when we were still powerless, Christ died for the ungodly."*[30] (Romans 5:6) This liberating truth is the power to lift our eyes off ourselves and our self-effort (religion) and onto Christ, for it is only in beholding Him that we are being changed from glory to glory (2 Corinthians 3:18).

When the prodigal son told his father that he was no longer worthy to be called his son but instead should be reduced to a servant, he was asking to be defined by what he did. It is significant that the father does not negotiate with his son. He refuses to even dignify the suggestion with an answer but instead turns to speak to his servants. His first word is *"Quick!"*[31] (Luke 15:22). O that His Church would be as alert and steadfast today in refusing to mix our works with our identity (Galatians 5:1). The gospel that declares, *"Since, then, you have been raised with Christ,"*[32] (Colossians 3:1) the gospel of the new creation, where old things have passed away and all things have become new, cannot be mixed with the Law. When the Church tolerates a mixed message of grace and law, she is saying to the Father in effect, "We are not worthy to be called by the name *son*, to be 'in Christ,' to find our being with you. Make us servants. Name us after our works and let us earn our being with you. Let us

---

[30] New International Version.
[31] New International Version.
[32] New International Version.

name ourselves after our works: our repentance, our obedience, and our prayer life. Let us live always becoming but never being, never being 'with you,' until all that we owe you we have sufficiently 'paid back.'"

To the natural man this 'gospel' of good living seems eminently reasonable (1 Corinthians 2:14). This is because his fallen vision cannot conceive of a god who is not as self-centred as he is! He cannot conceive of a salvation where he is not playing some central role. Our pride elevates us to the position of saviour and blinds us to the truth that a life apart from God is not life at all, but death, and dead men cannot save themselves (Ephesians 2:5). The gospel is not instruction on what we need to do that we may save ourselves. It is good news for the powerless! It is the revelation that at just the right time, when we were powerless to save ourselves, Christ died for us (Romans 5:6). It is not instruction on how we can become less sinful, that Christ may save us. It is the revelation of the love of God, His very nature, that has been demonstrated in this: that while we were *still* sinners, Christ died for us (Romans 5:8). Earthly religion says, "Do." The Gospel declares, "Done!"

Listen to how the prodigal son's plan of salvation still underestimates his own father. "*I will arise and go to my father and will say to him, "Father, I have sinned against heaven and before you, and I am no longer worthy to be called your son. Make me like one of your hired servants.*"[33] (Luke 15:18, 19). That prodigal son left home to make a name for himself, and here he is back again, still trying to name himself after his own life. He is living as an orphan. He thinks his greatest need is to know what to do. He is saying, in effect, "Father, instruct me on what I need to do, and I will do it. Be my instructor, my manager."

But the father sees immediately that his son's greatest need is not to know what to do, but to know who he is. His greatest need is not an instructor but a father. This is the love of God, the love that Jesus

---

[33] New King James Version.

was describing in the father running to embrace his stinking son. It is a love that didn't say, "First get yourself cleaned up and work off your debt, and then I will clothe you in my best and celebrate you." Rather, it is a love that knows that our deepest need is not for an instructor but a father (1 Corinthians 4:15), for we need a love that will not stand back from us but embrace us. In Christ we have received such a love (Romans 5:8, Romans 8:32). In Him is the revelation that we have a father who did not and cannot stand back from us, a father who did not leave us to save ourselves by giving us mere instruction, but a father who gave us nothing less than his own life (John 1:16-18).

I am not writing this book to point you to a life you should achieve, for to leave you looking to yourself would be to leave you looking in the wrong direction. Rather, I want to point us to the life we have been given, to the generosity of God, to the truth that we have a God who has held nothing back of Himself from us. *"He that spared not his own Son, but delivered him up for us all, how shall he not with him also freely give us all things?"*[34] (Romans 8:32).

I love to write this truth because I believe that the very proclamation of this good news is the power for us to believe and receive Him who has been freely given (Romans 1:16, Romans 10:17). I pray that as you read, you may find yourself as surprised as Saul of Tarsus by the grace of God. This is a gospel for the powerless. It is news of a Saviour in a world of instructors, and it is good news for all people, including atheists. (Luke 2:10). It is a gospel for the powerless, not a religion for the pious!

---

[34] King James Bible.

Chapter Three

Church begotten, not made. From eternal students to eternal sons.

· · · ·

I grew up in a happy and very busy family with three brothers and three sisters. As well as looking after her children, my mother was also trying to help my father run a business from our home. On any given morning, she could be the business' accountant, receptionist, veterinary nurse, and practice manager, all while getting seven children ready for school! Eventually Dad managed to persuade her to let him hire someone to come in and help her once a week. Mum had resisted this idea for a long time but finally agreed to have a lady called Margery come to our home every Wednesday to help with the housework. It all seemed like a great idea, except for one little flaw in Dad's plan. Every Tuesday night, Mum would work even harder to make sure the house was spotless for Margery's arrival!

Do you know a big reason why many people in our communities never darken the door of a church? They think they need to get their lives cleaned up *before* they come. If multitudes think they must reach a certain level of cleanliness *before* God will accept them, the tragic irony is that they probably got that idea from

Christians. Somehow over two thousand years, we managed to take a message that said, "Receive God's acceptance of you in Christ and be changed" and replace it with one that says, "You need to change in order for God to accept you." The apostle John used two words that forever clarify that God is the author of salvation: "He first!" *"We love Him, because He first loved us."*[35] (1 John 4:19).

The gospel is not a message about what God can do for you *if* you only get yourself cleaned up a bit. Newsflash! He didn't come to help you clean your house. He came to demolish your house, for in Christ you died, and your life is hidden with Christ in God (Colossians 3:3). The gospel is not 'Get your act together,' for your 'act' ended the moment Jesus died. As He cried out, *"It is finished,"* the huge curtain in the temple, representing the separation of a holy God from unholy men, was torn in two from top to bottom. That was literally the curtain coming down on your act and mine! Exit stage left, Act 1: the old Adamic life of man trying to save himself. There then followed a short intermission of three days, while all of creation sat on the edge of their seats for Act 2. This too started with a curtain being rolled away, a curtain of stone. The resurrected Jesus, the Last Adam, emerges onto the stage in a blinding flash of light, brighter than the sun, and there opens before mankind a new and living way, the life in union with God through Jesus Christ. *"We throw open our doors to God and discover at the same moment that he has already thrown open his door to us"*[36] (Romans 5:2).

This is the God we worship. He is not the God who left us to save ourselves, for He is love, and love cannot be content with sending a message. Love comes in person. The apostle John said it this way: *"For the law was given by Moses, but grace and truth came by Jesus Christ."*[37] (John 1:17). God forbid, but if a child of yours lay dying in the hospital, would you be content with sending a message?

---

[35] New King James Version.
[36] The Message.
[37] The King James Bible.

What would you think of a parent who decided just to send their child a text message or a letter? The love in your heart for your own child would compel you to come in person. If we know how to give good gifts to our children, how much more does our Father in heaven give His Spirit to all who look to Him? (Matthew 7:11). God pours out His love into our hearts by the gift of His Holy Spirit, that we may glimpse the truth about 'Our Father who art in heaven.'

It bears repeating: in Jesus' parable of the prodigal son, the father did not dress his son to convince himself that this beggar before him is his son, but to convince the son! It is the son who judges himself by his behaviour and thinks he doesn't deserve to live as a son (Luke 15:19). The father had never thought that way. His name for his son, his 'call' on him, had never changed, for the Father never saw the son's life as born from what he did, but as born from Him (John 1:13).

When we were all infants, we behaved no better than dogs. We would have happily eaten our food off the floor, done our business on the floor, and howled when we wanted to be fed! Why then did our parents not just treat us according to our behaviour and rear us as a dog? Because they were absolutely persuaded of two truths: that we were their child, and that if we were to grow up to be whom they saw us to be, we needed to be treated as their child every day, irrespective of our behaviour!

This is why the apostle Paul, who called himself their spiritual father, wrote to the Corinthians when he heard they were living in gross immorality and addressed them as saints and *"the temple of God"* (1 Corinthians 3:16). Outwardly it appeared that these Christians had a 'sinning' problem, but Paul knew that the root of their behaviour was a 'seeing' problem. In their hearts they were perceiving themselves to be mere men and so were living out those beliefs (1 Corinthians 3:3). They were grasping for life because they had forgotten (or never perceived) that life in all its fullness had already been given to them in Christ (1 Corinthians 3:21, 22). What they needed was not mere instruction on how to behave better, but a spiritual father or mother. They needed someone who knew them after the spirit, who knew them to be children born of God, and who also knew that they could only grow up as sons of God by being spoken to not according to their behaviour, but according to their heavenly calling. This required a love that could see through their outward appearance, a love that could see past their past, no matter how repulsive. In the words of Paul, they needed a father, not an instructor, as they already had far too many instructors (1 Corinthians 4:15).

If many of us in the modern church have also struggled to mature into the image of Christ, might it be that we are suffering the same excess of instruction and dearth of spiritual fathering? If our hearts have grown sick and weary as believers, there may be a simple reason for that. We have been hearing far too much instruction on what we need to do to become and not enough Gospel to empower us to *be*. We are simply discovering again that there is no power in any message that points us to ourselves. Instruction is beneficial, but only when we are pointed to Christ as our life, not our obedience. (Romans 10:2-4) The Gospel is news, not advice. It 'begets' life. (1 Corinthians 4:15). But if we keep preaching instruction each week rather than gospel, then we will continue to find in our churches the best-educated orphans in the kingdom, always becoming but never being the sons of God (John 14:18, Ephesians 4:14, 15).

To be filled with the love of our heavenly father for his children, to be filled with his spirit, is to find in yourself the capacity to see past a person's behaviour and perceive the call of God on their life—the person He sees them to be in Him. God sees past our past! To serve Him, we need to be able to do the same: see past our own past and those of others. For this, we need to be filled with the Spirit of Him who sees past our past.

This was the vision that rose up in a Christian called Ananias and empowered him to walk up to Saul of Tarsus, the great persecutor of the Church, and address him as '*brother* Saul' (Acts 9:10-18). Ananias, full of the Holy Spirit, saw past Saul's past and saw his destiny in Christ. We could say it was the heart of a spiritual father who called forth Paul out of Saul.

The apostle Paul described such a birthing as *"I have begotten you through the gospel."*[38] (1 Corinthians 4:15). In this sense the body is like the head (Christ), as the Church too shares in a life 'begotten not made.' Our thinking needs to be renewed daily, that we may grow up into the reality of our sonship in Christ. But any lack of such growth does not negate the truth of what our life *is*. Our life *is* hidden with Christ in God (Colossians 3:3), and you and I can say with Paul, *"by the grace of God I am what I am."*[39] (1 Corinthians15:10) The Holy Spirit is not in the business of persuading our hearts of who we could be, but of who we are. (Romans8:16)

In Luke 15, Jesus tells us that the prodigal son had a plea, a rehearsed prayer to his father that he was pinning all his hopes on to save his life. It went like this: *"I am no longer worthy to be called your son; make me like one of your hired servants."*[40] (Luke 15:21) Listen again to what he is saying: "I am no longer worthy to *be*." He is saying, "I want to draw back from the name you would give me, "Son". I want to be named according to what I have done, so give me the name '*servant*.'

The danger with congregations remaining under ministry that is heavy on instruction on how to become better Christians is that their revelation of who they *now* are is being supplanted by one of who they might be, one day, if ... But how can they grow up in the reality of their *present* union with Christ if that union is continually presented to them as a conditional future event? It is good to study to show yourself approved, but Christ did not die to become the firstborn among many students but many brothers and sisters (Romans8:29). Our gatherings were not meant to be an eternal lecture theatre that one day we can graduate

---

[38] New King James Version.
[39] New King James Version.
[40] New International Version.

from, but rather to be places of celebration and supernatural joy as we perceive that He has already qualified us to share in His Kingdom (Colossians1:12). He calls us to a higher calling than eternal students. He calls us His eternal sons (Romans 8:14-17, 2 Timothy 1:9).

To grow up into the reality of who He has called us to be, we need to be spoken to as those who have already passed from death to life (John 5:24). Ministry that raises sons of God does not speak to them of a future promotion for good behaviour, but calls them to look up by the Spirit to see that their life has already been promoted to glory through the death and resurrection of Christ (Colossians 3:1-4). What higher life can there be than the one that begins at our participation in Christ's resurrection? This is what the apostle Peter meant when he said that God, the Father of our Lord Jesus Christ, *"has given us new birth into a living hope through the resurrection of Jesus Christ from the dead"*[41] (1 Peter 1:3). This was also where Paul began with his disciples, for the revelation of the Church's union with Christ was precisely where Christ began with Paul on the road to Damascus (Acts 9:4, 5).

Here is the great difference between the Gospel of Jesus Christ and every earthly religion. They all hold out the hope of acceptance with God (depending on your life). The Gospel declares acceptance in Christ not as our possible end, but as our sure foundation, our beginning. Unless we begin with the Father qualifying us through Christ, we have no beginning at all! This is why Paul refers to the resurrection of Christ from the dead as our justification (Romans 4:25) and that without it, we remain *"dead in sins"*[42] (Ephesians 2:5). Is it not amazing that we have so reduced the heavenly gospel to an earthly religious message that most Christians now see their behaviour as their hope of heaven, rather than the resurrection of Christ (1 Peter 1:3).

---

[41] New International Version.
[42] King James Bible.

Those of us who have been given the privilege of spiritual leadership in the Church carry a great responsibility for the words we speak over God's children. For us to see the spiritual growth of our congregations, from eternal students to eternal sons by the power of the Gospel, let us speak to them *"not after the flesh,"* for *"if anyone is in Christ, he is a new creation; old things have passed away; behold, all things have become new."*[43] (2 Corinthians 5:16,17). It is not the promise of the sun that makes the darkness flee but the presence of the sun. Let Christ be acknowledged in our midst, that the communication of our faith in this world becomes effective, for we are the light of the world because of His life *in* us, not our life for Him (Philemon 1:6).

If we are truly speaking to those who have already died and been resurrected in Christ, then let every instruction we give them be prefaced by these words, *"Therefore, since you have been raised with Christ ..."*[44] (Colossians3:1). Again, it is not the promise of the dawn that dispels the darkness but the presence of the dawn, and in Christ we are the light of the world (Matthew 5:14,15). Jesus said that our light cannot remain under a bushel (a dry measure). You see, the confidence to come boldly before the throne of grace and to shine like a city on a hill does not grow in a measuring environment. In such an atmosphere of deferred hope (where we appear to be in training to become sons one day), our hearts only grow sick (Proverbs13:12). Our hearts were built to celebrate, not endlessly calculate. The Father's house (His Church) should be full of the sound of a finished work (1 Kings 6:7) and the sound of music and dancing (Luke 15:25), for all work and no celebration indeed makes the Church a very dull son. How heaven must wonder that those called to shine brighter than the sun seem to have so settled in the shadows that 'churches' can now blend right into the high street with all the other 'advice centres' in town!

---

[43] New King James Version.
[44] Berean Standard Bible.

Keep watering down the Good News of what *He* has done with a little good advice on what *we* still need to do, and the result is that too many of us as believers struggle to see ourselves as who we now *are* in Christ (who we *are* in the Father's eyes), for we are being reared on the vision of who we are in our elder brother's eyes! Such short-sightedness is the result of our vision being formed by the words of those who see us primarily as workers *for* His Kingdom, rather than sons *in* His Kingdom. To be short-sighted in the Spirit is to be living as if what Christ achieved wasn't enough to qualify us to live in communion with His Spirit (2 Peter 1:9). When the blind lead the blind, the only way is down, and how the angels must wonder at the sight of sons of God living as mere men (1 Corinthians 3:3). It was in the first Adam that we fell, from being to becoming. But in the last Adam (Christ), we rose, from becoming to being, being with Christ in God (Colossians 3:3).

An instructor (manager) can tell you what to do, but a father tells you who you are.

Only the words of a father can impart what a manager cannot: a revelation of identity that transcends earthly performance; the life of a son, not the life of an employee working his way to a promotion! When believers come to see that they are a Christian not because of their new behavior but because of their new birth, that they are saved by grace through faith, and this not of themselves (Ephesians 2:3, 9), a remarkable thing happens. They finally stop *trying* to be a Christian and start living as a child of God. They begin to see themselves as their Father sees them: hidden with Christ in God (Colossians 3:3). To see yourself the way the Father sees you is to be filled with a joy inexpressible and full of glory (1 Peter 1:8), and any believer full of such thanksgiving is holier accidentally than the most sin-conscious, self-absorbed zealot (Romans 10:1-4).

Irrespective of whether He finds them returning from the world stinking of drink or working away in the church stinking of self-righteousness, the Father always greets His children in the same way: as the apple of His eye, a cause for rejoicing (Luke 15:20-24).

Phelim Doherty

Only a gospel that reveals such a loving father can raise children who live so well loved that they speak the language of heaven in all circumstances—thanksgiving—and by this the will of the Father is done on the earth (1 Thessalonians 5:16-18). Perfectly loved children reveal a perfectly loving father. Students are a testimony to their teacher. But sons are a testimony of their father.

Chapter Four

The Father who never left us to save ourselves.

• • • •

Growing up with three brothers and three sisters presented some challenges to going on a family holiday. Perhaps that is why I remember so well an incident from one of the rare occasions we found ourselves together at a resort. It was in the county of Waterford, in what is called the 'sunny southeast' of Ireland (I think they use the term 'sunny' in a relative sense!). There we came across a lake where you could hire rowing boats, and one of my sisters immediately asked our father for permission to go out in one of the boats with one of my brothers. They were both very young and had never rowed a boat before. Much to our amazement, Dad said yes, and the rest of us watched rather nervously as they somehow managed to manoeuvre their craft out to the middle of the lake. It was all too good to last. As suddenly as that storm had descended on Jesus' boat on the Sea of Galilee, so the inevitable argument broke out about whose turn it was to row, and in the ensuing struggle the oars fell into the water. Panic ensued, and they both began shouting and crying out for help at the top of their voices, convinced they were about to drown. But then a miracle! Something happened that caused them both to immediately go silent and sit there perfectly quiet and at peace and not a little mortified. One of the men hiring the boats just stepped into the lake in a pair of waders and walked right out to their boat. The water was only up to his knees! Without a word he took hold of the bow of their craft and walked back to the pier, just pulling it behind him. On seeing him approach, all my brothers' and sister's grasping to save themselves ceased, and the cries of their flesh were silenced. The truth had finally dawned: our father had never left them in a place where they would have to save themselves!

Only when your heart and mine are persuaded of the same—that our heavenly Father has not left us to save ourselves—will our attempts to save ourselves through our own piety be put to rest. Only that revelation of how well we have been saved delivers us from all the grasping of a world lusting for life (2 Peter 1:4). The Gospel declares a God who has not left us by ourselves to save ourselves. It declares, in effect, "Behold Christ, the power of God and the wisdom of God, for God never believed you could save yourself, so He never left you to save yourself. Jesus Christ, His life, death, resurrection, and ascension, *is* God not leaving you to save yourself!"

The power of the Gospel is found in the presence of the God of the Gospel, not in the eloquence of the message (1 Corinthians 2:1-5). Jesus had the capacity to compose the most persuasive of motivational messages, but He refused to say any more than He was hearing, for He came to serve His Father, not himself (John 12:49, Matthew 4:4).

Some time ago I was preparing a message for a Sunday morning service and had just written the words *"Imagine God saying this to you"* when I felt the Holy Spirit wanted me to look again at those words. I knew He wanted me to think again before making that statement, but I could not understand what was wrong with what I had written. In my heart I was saying, "What's wrong with that statement, Lord?" Within a few moments my heart heard this reply. "I did not give you my Spirit so that you could tell people to 'imagine' me speaking to them. I gave you my Spirit so that I could speak to them!"

We have not been given God's Spirit merely to tell people about God. We are filled with His Spirit that *He* would speak to people through us. To hear *of* God is different from hearing *about* God, and it is in this knowledge *of* God that His grace and peace are multiplied to us (2 Peter 1:2), for His voice empowers us to be whom He declares us to be (John 10:27, 28). He does not leave us to save ourselves, for He never believed we could do anything by ourselves. (John 15:5).

Faith is the language God speaks, for He is fully persuaded that your behaviour may change your opinion of who you are, but it doesn't change His! That's because you were never called according to your earthly record, but according to God's grace and purpose given in Christ long before you had done anything good or bad (2 Timothy 1:8, 9). The gospel on earth as it is in heaven is the call of the heart of the Father for His children. By His call we are empowered to be whom He sees us to be, for the very faith to be, comes in the call (Romans 1:16, 10:17). Through His call we find our 'being' in Him (Acts 17:28). We don't *become* sons of God by our religious efforts. We are who we are by the grace of God, and it is the gift of His Spirit that empowers us to be whom His Word declares us to be (1 Corinthians 15:10, Romans 8:16).

Adam in the garden of Eden believed a lie: that he could *become* like God by what he did. In the first Adam, we all fell, from being to becoming. But the last Adam (Christ) did not receive the lie that He could become like God by what He did. From the desert (Matthew 4:3) to the Cross (Mark 15:30, 31) Jesus refused all temptations to do something to save Himself. In His *being* as a man, He remained 'with God' (John 5:19, John 17:21) even unto death. Thus, in the last Adam, we rose, from becoming to being.

The Kingdom of the Son is the realm of what now is! In heaven, there is no one trying to *become* anyone, for all have found their *being* with God (Colossians 3:1-4). The kingdom of heaven is not the realm of becoming; it is the realm of being, the realm of the 'I am' (Exodus 3:14, John 8:58). In the Kingdom of God, to speak with authority is to speak knowing whom you are of (John 12:49), for the Gospel is not a message about filling heaven with orphans but filling the earth with sons.

This is why Jesus does not describe the prodigal son as having to spend years working his way back to his father's table. He is not a son because he can atone for his past. He is a son by birth. At no point in Jesus' parable is he becoming a son; he *is* a son. Repentance is not a work that 'earns' us the right to be accepted by God. Biblical repentance (metanoia) is a profound change of belief. It is not self-generated but the gift of God's Spirit that comes through the gospel of His grace. In that sense it is not 'of ourselves.' (Ephesians 2:8, 9. Romans 10:14, 15. Acts 11:18). When believers come to see this, they rise, from becoming to being. They stop *trying* to be a Christian and start living as sons of God (the term 'sons' encompasses both male and female believers as it speaks of their inheritance in Christ). Now, of course, sons must grow up to maturity, but that is not 'becoming' a son; that is being a son, a growing son (Ephesians 4:11-16, 1 John 2:12-14).

This 'coming to see' the New Testament describes as '*to be renewed in the spirit of your mind*'[45] (Ephesians 4:23). It is a maturing of the believer from a self-conscious to a God-conscious life. It is to find that I, who was once grasping for life, now find *His* life springing up in me. As we have already seen, this was Jesus' promise to the Samaritan woman at the well and to all who will receive Him as their life (John 4:14). Jesus is not the life-demander; He is the life-giver! Even the faith to believe in Him, is *from* Him (Romans 10:17).

This persuasion of the heart is a work of grace by God's Spirit, who pours the love of God into our hearts and witnesses with us that we *are* the children of God, not candidates for children if we pass the interview! (Romans 5:5, 8:16). Thus, by His Spirit, we rise from

---

[45] King James Bible.

becoming to being, and through this rising, God's being is seen in us (Luke 1:78, 79; 2 Peter 1:19). As the Son rises on us, our eyes are opened by the illumination of His Spirit to the fatherhood of God in the face of Christ (2 Corinthians 4:6). We perceive that we are sons, not orphans, and find ourselves transformed into His image with ever-increasing glory (2 Corinthians 3:18). We find ourselves living and moving and having our being in Him (Acts 17:28). We find ourselves 'like Him' (Colossians 3:4, 1 John 3:2). It is this maturing into His image that causes the Church to shine brighter and brighter with the glory of God; the set-apart life, for in a world darkened by the fear of death, the life not looking to save itself shines apart (Philippians 2:15). The more this revelation of our sonship in Christ rises in us, the brighter our lives reveal His glory, for "*…anything that is illuminated becomes a light itself*"[46] (Ephesians 5:13)

In a world full of marching armies, where every cause and movement seeks to flaunt their strength on the streets by force of numbers, the Church is called to reveal a different strength, one that lays down its life for others. In the first centuries of the Church, there were marches of Christians through cities that so deeply impacted their communities that many joined them and turned to Christ. What they witnessed was not a grasping for earthly power, but the manifestation of another kingdom entirely, one that death had no hold over. What they saw and heard were Christians being marched through the streets to the arena to be killed. The sound of their singing and the peace on their faces was like the inbreaking of the Kingdom of Heaven into the earth, for their eyes were fixed on a different kingdom and a different king (Acts 16:24, 25).

It was such a sight that haunted Saul of Tarsus on his way to Damascus. He had seen something that he could not unsee, and what he saw began to work at him and in him, and he found it hard to kick against it (Acts 26:14). He saw the face of a Christian being killed, and it was as the face of an angel, full of grace and

---

[46] Berean Standard bible.

peace. He watched Stephen die beholding the face of God, and that sight changed Saul (Acts.6:15, Acts 7:55-60), and Saul changed his generation.

Here is an evangelistic calling not many of us want to sign up for: how to die well! How to see everything you have worked for be taken from you and in that moment be filled with the peace of God, because you know that in Christ this world can take nothing from you. (Acts 7:54-60, Acts 9:5, Romans 8:37-39).

The witness of the Church is not the strength of our numbers but the strength of His life in us, the life that transcends the fears of this world, the life that does not seek to preserve itself, but lays down its life for others, the life that has already passed from death to life, from separation to union (Colossians 3:1-4). Such is the witness of the Church: that we live from union in a world of separation, from victory in a world of victims, for in Christ we live the life that gives, not the life that grasps (Philippians 2:6).

To speak to people as if there is something they must do, alone, apart from God, *before* God can do something for them, is to effectively tell people that they could become like God if only they tried harder! But we no more have the power within us to produce a life like God's than Mary had the power to 'produce' Christ. That's why the angel did not ask Mary to produce Christ but promised her that it would be by the Spirit of God that she would 'bear' Christ (Luke 1:34, 35) The whole world may be asking you to produce a good life, but God is not. That's because He didn't design us to *produce* life, but to *partake* of life (2 Peter 1:4). Jesus said it like this. *"I am the vine, you are the branches; the one who remains in Me, and I in him bears much fruit, for apart from Me you can do nothing."*[47] (John 15:5).

Imagine a branch of a tree saying to the tree, "What do you think is God's will for my life?" Would the tree not be entitled to say, "Your life? Listen, mate, apart from me, you don't have a life!" It may

---

[47] New American Standard Bible.

shock you to learn that God can no more help you to live *your* life, than you could help a child of yours to live as if you don't exist. His life in you *is* His will for your life, for this is what true love does: gives itself away. God doesn't love you because He needs something from you, and so His love is not conditional on your record. True love "*is not self-seeking*" and "*keeps no record of wrongs*" (1 Corinthians 13:5). In the words of the apostle Paul to the Romans, "*He who did not spare His own Son, but delivered Him up for us all, how shall He not with Him also freely give us all things?*"[48] (Romans 8:32).

This news is so wonderful, that it carries the power to drive out the fear in our lives that has always thrown us back on ourselves (1 John 4:18). The Lord knows that it is our attempts to save ourselves that cause us to hurt those who get close to us. If you dived into a river to rescue someone from drowning, you would not be surprised that their thrashing and grasping for life might hurt you. So too, as Jesus looked down from the cross on those killing Him, He cried out, "Father, *forgive them, for they don't know what they are doing.*"[49] (Luke 23:34). He was looking at us!

I can understand now that it was the way I was hearing the gospel that explains why it appeared powerless to transform me. I was hearing the gospel as good *advice*, not good *news*. I was hearing it as a message about what God needed *me* to do for Him, rather than one of what *He* had done for me. I was hearing it as a message of what *might be* if I, rather than as an announcement of what *is* because He.

In other words, I was hearing the Gospel as a message that pointed to me and my life, rather than one that pointed to Christ and His life. This was the reason that my life was not being filled with the transformative spirit of thanksgiving and joy that is carried by the gospel, for there is simply no power in any message that points you to yourself. (Galatians 3:2-14). If you think about it, the whole

---

[48] New King James Version.
[49] New Living Translation.

world is pointing you to yourself. From the phone in your pocket to your TV, you are being bombarded with information as never before. We are all being advised as never before, on what we need to do or buy if we are to have a better life. If I had to sum up this underlying message that every authority in this world wants us to hear, it would be, "Here is what you need to do to save yourself." You see a world that doesn't know a Saviour can only teach you to be your own! Unfortunately, if I am trying to save myself and you are trying to save yourself and the whole world is doing the same, then we end up with a very self-ish world.

So, what can save you and I from our selfishness? I will let the apostle Paul give you the answer: *"For I am not ashamed of the gospel, because it is the power of God that brings salvation to everyone who believes"*[50] (Romans 1:16). The Gospel is the good announcement that God has *not* left us to save ourselves, for Jesus Christ—His birth, life, death, resurrection, and ascension—is God not leaving us to save ourselves. In the words of Paul to the Ephesians, *"For it is by grace you have been saved, through faith—and this is not from yourselves, it is the gift of God—not by works, so that no one can boast."*[51] (Ephesians 2:8, 9). It seems that once we forget that salvation is *'not of ourselves,'* we are only left with the misery of being our own saviour. How miserable religion is, for self-effort can never match the joy of the gospel, for how will you ever know you have done enough to save yourself? Religion will leave you always becoming, but never being.

If you want a Saviour, you have one. If you still want to be your own, then there is religion or atheism. But be warned, it is the most miserable life in the world being your own saviour and all your grasping for life will only end up hurting those closest to you.

As you are reading these words, I pray that you may be aware of something stirring in your heart, even something like a weight

---

[50] New International Version.
[51] New International Version.

being lifted from your mind. That will be the burden of trying to save yourself. That weight is crushing you. God is not asking you to produce faith by yourself. Faith is the gift of God that comes by hearing the message about Christ (Romans 10:17), and it brings your heart to rest. It was Saint Augustine who famously said, "You have made us for yourself, O Lord, and our hearts are restless until they rest in You".

Deep down in your soul you already know, that even if you manage one day to achieve all the goals that this world promises will give you a great life, you will wake up the following morning to find yourself still not satisfied. This is because you have a thirst in you for life that this world cannot satisfy (John 4:13, 14). You weren't made to produce life, but to partake of life, and that life is freely gifted to you in Christ—life with God, the God who took your sin and death into Himself so that you could receive His eternal life as your own (Romans 6:10, 11; 2 Corinthians 5:19).

Being told what you need to do, never sets anyone free, because being pointed to yourself can never set you free from yourself. You needed a Saviour to set you free, and you are not that Saviour. That's because we have a father who never left us to save ourselves. That is not advice; that is news!

Chapter Five

Brighter than the Sun: The Extravagance of God.

● ● ● ●

Extravagant: "exceeding the limits of reason or necessity, lacking in moderation, balance, and restraint."[52]

Have you ever heard the old tale about a very strange auction that takes place in the grounds of a large mansion? The owner had recently passed away and had no children to inherit his estate. All his most precious belongings had been laid out on the lawn before his house, and many wealthy people had gathered, eager to bid on these valuable items. The first item to be put up for auction is an old painting of the owner's son. His son had passed away many years before, and few present that day had ever met or even heard of him. As the auctioneer repeatedly asked for bids, there was only silence. Some began to get irritated, wanting him to accept that no one wanted the painting and move on to more valuable items.

But that morning the estate's head gardener also happened to be in the grounds, still lovingly tending the plants and shrubs as he had for many years. He was old enough to remember the owner's son, who had died tragically as a young man. He also knew of the

---

[52] https://www.merriam-webster.com/dictionary/extravagant

great love the father had for his son and how precious this painting was to him. Grieved that everyone appeared to be rejecting the item, the gardener put up his hand and bought the painting for a small sum. Immediately upon that purchase, the auctioneer announced that the sale was now over, and that the entire estate was now the legal property of the gardener. In reply to a barrage of complaints and questions, he produced a copy of the will of the owner and read out his wishes. It contained only one stipulation. Whoever bought the painting would inherit all his estate. Whoever got the son, got everything!

Here is the extravagance of the gospel. Whoever gets the Son, gets everything.

You get His faith, His holiness, His obedience, His past and His future, and His life! (Galatians 2:20, 1 Corinthians 1:30, Romans 5:19, Colossians 3:1-4). That's why to have the Son, is to have passed from death to life (John 5:24). Yet we have been left in a world overshadowed by death, for this world needs light, and God has chosen to shine His extravagance through us (Matthew 5:14-16, Ephesians 5:8, Philippians 2:15). It was through believing the original lie that God was withholding Himself from us (Genesis 3:4), that man was cast down into the darkness of sin and death. Christ has now appeared as the truth about God's extravagance (John 1:17, 18), so that in believing in His true extravagance towards us, Jesus Christ, we may find ourselves living again in the light of the truth: that we have a generous father, not a frugal manager. We are given God's Spirit to enable us to be so persuaded that we are indeed the children of such a generous father, that our lack of fear of death lights up a world living in the fear of death (Hebrews 2:15). We should be so unafraid of losing our lives, that we live the most extravagant of lives, the life of Christ.

This book is not about how God could be more extravagant to you, if only you tried a bit harder to be a better person. My message is that God *is* extravagant. He can't help it, and He can't stop it. It *is* who He is, and I believe His Spirit is given to us that we may perceive who He *is* and declare who He *is*, and in knowing who He *is*, find ourselves knowing who we are in Him (1 John 3:2). Thus, to preach in the power of the Spirit, is to declare what *is* because Christ lives, not what might be if you live holy enough for long enough! This is why the Word of God does not say that the Spirit witnesses with our spirits that we might be the children of God, or could be, or should be, but that we are! Romans 8:16 declares, *"The Spirit himself testifies with our spirit that we are God's children."*[53] This is such an extravagant claim that the apostle John marvelled at what that meant about the character of God. *"See what great love the Father has lavished on us, that we should be called children of God! And that is what we are! The reason the world does not know us is that it did not know him."*[54] (1 John 3:1)

But here is the most wonderful thing, the most extravagant thing. Whereas men in their earthly wisdom will only call you a child of God when you are behaving as one, I have come to understand (after years of trying and failing to become a good Christian), that a love that is conditional on my behaviour, is not strong enough to change my behaviour. I need a love that lays down its life for me while I am still spitting in its face and crucifying it. Only in Jesus Christ do I find a love like that, a love stronger than the love I find in all the religions of this world. To them, God will meet you in the holy place of the temple or the church building, for they have a god who wants to meet you at your best. But we have a God who meets us at our worst, whose Spirit will find you in the pigpen or in the gutter and will speak to you there and call you, *"...not according to our works, but according to His own purpose and grace which was given to us in Christ Jesus before time began."*[55] (2 Timothy. 1:9,10) Just ask Abraham, or Moses, or Gideon, or David, or Mary, or any of the patriarchs or prophets if

---

[53] New International Version.
[54] New International Version.
[55] New King James Version.

they thought their record qualified them for the high call of God on their lives; the name He was calling them by.

While the whole world is still berating you to get your act together *before* God will accept you, the Holy Spirit will not, for He is not here to point you to you, but to point you to Christ. How does the Holy Spirit persuade you that you are a new creation in Christ? Simple. He never speaks to you as if you are not!

While everyone who only sees you by your earthly record wants to speak to you of what you must do to get your act together, the Holy Spirit can only speak to you as if the curtain came down on your act two thousand years ago, because it did! (Matthew 27:51). Here is the good news of the Gospel: you have a Saviour. Now again, if you still want to be your own, there is religion or atheism. But be warned, it is the most miserable life in the world being your own saviour, for atheism will give you no hope and religion will give you no rest!

Your behaviour doesn't make God more generous towards you. You don't make Him who He is. In fact, He never wanted any of us to live thinking that His love was shackled to our behaviour, which is why He chose exactly the right time to give us all He could give. He gave His very life to us not when we were powerfully good, but when we were powerless to do good (Romans 5:6-8).

This truth, that our salvation does not arise from our goodness but Christ's, remains at the heart of Jesus' most well-known parable, the story of the prodigal son. Listen again to the first thing Jesus says about the father in that story. *"And he said, A certain man had two sons: And the younger of them said to his father, Father, give me the portion of goods that falleth to me. And he divided unto them his living."*[56] (Luke 15:11, 12) Often when we read this parable, we think of the Father's generosity as appearing at the end of the story, in the great feast He provides. It is almost as if the father's extravagance is something both sons had to work towards, and indeed they both

---

[56] King James Bible.

believed it was! (Luke 15:17-19, 29, 30) But the word translated there as "his living" is the Greek word 'Bios'. 'It literally means *"life; that is the present state of existence."*[57] Here is the Father pouring out His living, His life, at the beginning of the story, not the end.

The extravagance of God is also where our story begins, not ends, for in speaking of Christ the Bible describes Him as *"the Lamb slain from the foundation of the world."*[58] (Revelation 13:8). When it comes to God's extravagance, His generosity, and His love, these are not rewards that come at the end of our story, one day in heaven. Our story begins with the extravagant generosity of a Father who made us for one purpose: that He could *so* love us, as to give us His very own life. That in receiving His life (in the gift of His Son), we would no longer perish in the far country our own grasping hearts had led us to, but could be led to faith by the light of the gospel, in the same way that the prodigal son was led home by the remembrance of His Father's generosity (John 3:16).

Here is the good news of the gospel: you don't have to move God to be generous to you.

It is not our repentance that makes God's generosity extravagant. It is the revelation of His extravagant generosity that causes us to repent (Romans 2:4). The root meaning of that word 'repent' (*Metanoia*) is "to think differently"[59] It is to experience a fundamental change in what we believe, and it is from such an extravagant change of beliefs that we begin to think differently and so act differently. The things we do, good or bad, are only the branches of our life. The root is what our hearts are believing (Proverbs 4:23). Again, Jesus came to take an axe to the root, not the branches. That is why He said to the religious teachers who were obsessed with people's behaviour, *"Blind Pharisee, first cleanse the inside of the cup and dish, that the outside of them may be clean also."*[60] (Matthew 23:26). And it

---

[57] Strongs Number G979.
[58] New King James Version.
[59] Strongs Number 3340
[60] New King James Version.

is why, when asked by people, *"What must we do to do the works of God?* His reply was, *"This is the work of God, that you believe in Him whom He sent."*[61] (John 6:29). He was saying, in effect, "Believe in God's way of saving you, not your own!"

True repentance, therefore, is only possible when we *see* how well we have been saved in Jesus Christ. Only a revelation from the Holy Spirit of the extravagance of God in giving us His Son, can set our hearts at rest. Because it is only when we *see* how well we have been saved, that we can finally stop grasping in this world to save ourselves, for *"He who did not spare His own Son, but delivered Him up for us all, how shall He not with Him also freely give us all things?"*[62] (Romans 8:32).

Now if I want to go to the Word of God to give you more illustrations of the extravagance of God towards mankind, my problem is where to begin! The common place to begin is in the Garden of Eden, with God giving mankind the whole earth to be his domain, to rule over and prosper in (Genesis 1:28). But to begin to touch on the extravagance of God's generosity, we can do better than beginning with God giving man the earth, for as the first Adam showed us, indeed a man can gain the whole world and still lose his soul, his true life. (Matthew 16:26). I think to begin to see the extravagance of God (and that is all we ever can do is begin), we need to begin in another garden, the garden of Gethsemane. There we see God not just giving us His world, but giving us His life.

In that garden we see Him loving us enough to descend into the darkness of our condition, so much so that He began to sweat blood (Luke 22:44). He partook of the poverty of our loneliness that we could partake of the riches of His fellowship, the extravagance of the love found in the Father, Son, and Holy Spirit, which is their very nature (1 John 4:8). The best god an earthly mindset can come up with, is one who sits in heaven waiting to see who can qualify their

---

[61] New King James Version.
[62] New King James Version.

way to Him through the goodness of their lives. That is because, apart from God's extravagant Spirit, our earthly minds are too frugal and miserly to think or imagine a God so loving, that His way of loving us is not to stand back from us but to fall on our dirty lives and embrace us into Himself. Again, His way (Christ) is to embrace our lonely life and our lonely death, to go down with our ship so that the way could be made for us to rise up in His, the fellowship of the Father and the Son, in the Spirit. That way could never come from the religious works of men, but only come in the person of God in flesh, Emmanuel, God with us, the way, the truth, and the life of God, given to us.

When I begin to wonder about how much God entered the loneliness of our condition, I find myself thinking of Jesus in that garden rebuking Peter, James, and John for falling asleep (Matthew 26:40-45). As He began to experience the darkness of our death encroaching on Him, like a black sun rising, He began to experience new depths of our loneliness. During the storm on the Lake of Galilee, when those same disciples had expressed the darkness of the fear gripping their souls, Jesus had chided them on their lack of faith. On the day their boat appeared to be sinking, it was Jesus who slept and his disciples who woke him and questioned how He could sleep while they were in such need. (Mark 4:37, 38).

But now in the garden of Gethsemane, we see a God extravagant enough in His love to enter the darkness of our living death, our perishing condition. Now it is Jesus who finds Himself saying to His disciples, in effect, 'Why do you sleep? Don't you care?' (Matthew 26:40). Now it is His life that is sinking below waves of sorrow, overwhelmed to the point of death (Matthew 26:38), and it is He who cries out not to be left alone. Here is the light of God entering the depths of man's darkness. Here is the extravagance of a love that is fully entering into the depths of our perishing condition, our aloneness, that He may rescue us from the darkness we have fallen into.

This world is full of gods who offer us the world, even offer us heaven. Where in this world can we find a god extravagant enough to offer us Himself? Only in Christ do we see such a god of such extravagance—'exceeding the limits of reason or necessity, lacking in moderation, balance, and restraint,' for to lay down your life for the ones you love, is not an act of moderation, balance, or restraint.

I can do nothing with words but scratch the surface of the extravagance of God. Perhaps that is because one glimpse of His extravagance is so bright that we scarcely can take it in. On that road to Damascus, Saul of Tarsus got one glimpse of the goodness of God and described it as *"a light from heaven, brighter than the sun"*[63] (Acts 26:13), and he went blind. Perhaps that was a physical manifestation of a reality that had just gripped his heart: that in truth he was already completely blind to the goodness of God. In all his religious knowledge and experience of God, He never imagined or conceived of a god extravagant enough to so join his life to men, that He could say of His church, *"Saul, Saul, why do you persecute me?.. I am Jesus, whom you are persecuting."*[64] (Acts 9:4, 5).

For all our lives on this earth, this land of shadows, we will only be seeing the extravagance of God in part. That's not because God has withheld the fullness of His grace from us, but because our hearts have been so sickened by the frugal spirit of this world (Proverbs 13:12). The spirit of this world can only keep directing our gaze down onto ourselves, so much so, that we have got used to living in a twilight zone of God's extravagance (1 Corinthians 2:12). No wonder so many of us at first can only squint at the gospel of God's grace. Our lives are so overshadowed by death, that this knowing of God, this eternal life (John 17:3), His extravagant life, appears as a dawn brighter than the sun.

---

[63] New International Version.
[64] New International Version.

Chapter Six

When the Gospel dawns: Repentance toward God.

• • • •

Some years ago, on a visit to South Wales, I took the tour of an old coal mine. This involved descending several hundred feet in a lift into the bowels of the earth. As soon as we reached the bottom, the guide asked us to turn off all our helmet lights. The darkness was absolute, and the thought of working in such an environment with the constant danger of being trapped there was chilling. I learned on that tour that before the age of machines, ponies were employed to carry both coal and equipment through these tunnels. There were stables deep underground where some of these poor creatures lived between shifts. As they worked for periods of weeks or months underground, their eyes would get acclimatised to the poor light. But this meant that these animals could not be brought up to the surface during the day, as they could not have coped with the brightness of ordinary daylight and would have been very distressed. They would be brought up at night, and as the sun rose slowly, their eyes would have time to adjust to the strength of the light. For us too, the brightness of the goodness of God is something that dawns slowly on our souls (John 16:12, 2 Peter 1:19).

Not so, Saul of Tarsus! Poor Saul was brought up out of the darkness of his own religious pit so quickly that he couldn't stand it. The light blinded him (Acts 9:3-9). The funny thing is that we talk about people having "a road to Damascus" experience when we want to describe an instantaneous change of heart. But Acts 9 doesn't describe Saul of Tarsus having that sort of road to Damascus experience. Instead, it says he had to be led everywhere by the hand for three days until the Lord used a disciple called Ananias to pray for him. Only then did his sight return, as he was filled with the Holy Spirit. (Acts 9:17, 18). Saul was literally led to repentance. We have been given the Holy Spirit because blind men cannot lead themselves. They must be led.

True repentance is a profound change of heart, a change of belief, and this is not something we can produce in and of ourselves. We, too, need to be led to repentance. Later in his life, the apostle Paul spoke of this leading, in his letter to the Romans. *"Or do you think lightly of the riches of His kindness and restraint and patience, not knowing that the kindness of God leads you to repentance?"*[65] (Romans 2:4). The root meaning of the Greek word translated in that verse as "leads to" is defined as *"to lead by laying hold of, and this way to bring to the point of destination: of an animal"* or *"to lead with one's self, attach to one's self as an attendant."*[66] Let me say that in another way. The repentance that God brings, is to lead men and women to where He wants to bring them, by joining Himself to them and going with them! He has never been a god who stood back from us. From the incarnation to the day of Pentecost, He has been the God who has drawn near and joined Himself to us.

Think of Jesus drawing near the two disciples on the road to Emmaus, to walk with them, to join Himself to them, even as they walked in the wrong direction. As He spoke to them, their beliefs

---

[65] New American Standard Bible.
[66] Strongs Number G71 https://www.blueletterbible.org/lexicon/g71/kjv/tr/0-1/

were being changed utterly. They were being led to repentance, and it felt to them like their hearts were burning within them (Luke 24:13-32). Thank God His Spirit walks with us too, even in seasons when we are blind to His presence.

Jesus never stood at a distance shouting at people to repent. In Him the Kingdom of God drew near, bringing the power to repent, His very presence. (Matthew 4:17, Luke 10:9) He never left us to do anything by ourselves, even repent, for no part of our salvation is *"of ourselves"* (Ephesians 2:8, 9). Repentance is therefore not a matter of willpower but of our wills empowered by the presence of God. This is what is being expressed by Paul when he declares, *"I have been crucified with Christ, and I no longer live ..."*[67] (Galatians 2:20) Unfortunately, to earthly ears, statements such as "I repented. I believed. I turned away from my sin, I confessed Jesus as my Lord and Saviour" and "I am following Jesus" all appear to be pointing to the 'I,' the 'ego,' as the initiator, the author of my salvation. Such language is certainly familiar to earthly men, for all their lives they have lived with their whole world revolving around 'I.'. But the true extravagance of God is not seen in the life of 'I.'. It is seen in the death of 'I'!

It is fitting that a cross is an 'I' with a stroke through it. The message of Jesus Christ is not a religion for the pious, but a gospel for the powerless. It is good news, not mere good instruction, for no amount of instruction can help a dead man! (Romans 5:6, Ephesians 2:5). We rejoice because we were dead and are now alive, we were lost and are now found, but we didn't resuscitate ourselves, and lost sheep don't find the shepherd. We don't rejoice because we know how to get saved. We rejoice because we have a Saviour and He is not I! (Galatians 2:20)

Church, whatever you and I did, or prayed, we did by the grace of God, for apart from him we can do nothing, least of all comprehend His extravagance (1 Corinthians 2:9, 10). This is why "no *one can*

---

[67] New International Version.

say 'Jesus is Lord', except by the Holy Spirit."[68] (1 Corinthians 12:3). Apart from Him, we were dead, cut off from the life of God. We were perishing, and like all drowning men when He found us, we were grasping at everything and anything to save ourselves. We have a God extravagant enough to dive into what was killing us and wrap His body around ours. He is not the god of religion who waits on the shore promising he will pull us out, if we can swim well enough to get to him! The Bible is not a manual of swimming instructions. It is the revelation of a God so extravagant in His love, that He dives into our death, that He may raise us into His life.

True biblical repentance is not a work of our flesh, a work of man, but a work of God's Spirit. *'Metanoia'* encompasses much more than a turning *away* in the strength of our flesh from sin. It is a turning *to* God as He really *is*. But no man can see Him as He really is without a revelation of Christ by God's Spirit. This is why Paul declared to the Corinthians, *"no one can say that Jesus is Lord except by the Holy Spirit."*[69] (1 Corinthians 12:3), because *"No eye has seen, no ear has heard, and no mind has imagined what God has prepared for those who love him. But it was to us that God revealed these things by his Spirit. For his Spirit searches out everything and shows us God's deep secrets."*[70] (1 Corinthians 2:9, 10). How can a person truly turn to God, if they have not truly seen Him, not seen how good He really is? Only God's Spirit can reveal this to each person, and He delights to do so as the message of just how generous God is (Christ and Him crucified) is proclaimed (Romans 2:4).

How good is God? Good enough to save us, not when we were at our best but at our worst. *"But God demonstrates His own love toward us, in that while we were still sinners, Christ died for us."*[71] (Romans 5:8). In other words, to see God as He truly is, is to see that His love is not a self-seeking love. He is not loving us to get something from

---

[68] New International Version.
[69] New King James Version.
[70] New Living Translation.
[71] New King James Version.

us, but because He *is* love (1 John 4:8). When we speak of repentance or obedience or faith or love, I am not saying that we do not have to give God any of the above. I am saying that we *cannot* give God any of the above, unless His Spirit first rises on us, for "*we love Him because He first loved us.*"[72] (1 John 4:19).

True biblical repentance, then, is not something a man can work up from within himself, apart from a revelation of the goodness of God. For anyone to have a true metanoia, a repentance *unto* God (Acts 20:21), they first must see how good He is towards them when they were at their worst (Luke 22:61). Implicit in that statement, is the truth of our need to see the depth of our lack, if we are to appreciate the heights of His generosity. We cannot see His goodness in truth, if we have not seen our worst in truth. Yet a man brought up in complete darkness does not know what darkness even is, until light comes! (Matthew 4:16, 2 Corinthians 4:4) God never expected us to repent apart from His Spirit, His presence, for no human mind can ever imagine how good God is (1 Corinthians 2:9, 10). This is why, in speaking of Jesus going to live in Galilee, Matthew quotes the prophet Isaiah: "The *people living in darkness have seen a great light; on those living in the land of the shadow of death, a light has dawned.*"[73] (Matthew 4:16).

Notice this doesn't say that these people managed to produce some light themselves.

This is why it is so frustrating to see believers standing on street corners shouting at people to repent, in a way that implies that God can do nothing for them, until they first produce something for Him. But people cannot truly repent unto God, without a true revelation of God, and that revelation is Christ! Don't call on people to repent, if you have not proclaimed Christ to them. Would you stand on a riverbank shouting at a drowning man to repent, or would you give him something to take hold of, even your own body?

---

[72] New King James Version.

[73] New International Version.

Jesus Christ isn't God standing back from us and shouting 'Repent,' but God descending into what was killing us and putting His own body between us and death (1 Peter 2:24). He didn't do that while shouting at us, but did it without opening His mouth, as silently as a lamb going to the slaughter (Isaiah 53:7). It's not difficult to heap enough fear and condemnation on people, that they resolve to try harder to turn from their sins. But shouting at people to try harder to separate themselves from sin, isn't preaching Christ. It is preaching them!

Despite our earnestness, we all inevitably discover that there is no sustaining power in any message that points you to yourself (Galatians 3:5). Now you can certainly scare people into behaviour modification. They may stop their drinking, smoking, and cursing and even start attending religious services, but they do not have the power to change the self-centredness of their own heart. In their hearts they will believe that they saved themselves by what they did, and such a heart will always sit in judgment on others (Luke 15:28-30). Such a heart will also inevitably express the gospel as instruction, not news!

The life of Christ cannot be formed in us by the fear of rejection, for Christ's life was not raised on the fear of separation but on the faithfulness of His Father (Luke 2:49). Guilt, fear, and shame are the deadbeat dads of the spiritual world. They demand much, but supply nothing!

If we want people to truly repent, then we must proclaim the *evangelion*[74], the good announcement of what Christ has done about their sin, for Jesus did not just cry, 'Repent.' He declared, *"Repent, for the Kingdom of Heaven has drawn near."*[75] (Matthew 4:17). Don't expect people to repent if your words do not bring a revelation, an impartation, of the Kingdom of Heaven. Again, it

---

[74] Strongs Number 2098. https://www.blueletterbible.org/lexicon/g2098/kjv/tr/0-1/
[75] Berean Literal Bible.

is not the promise of the dawn that dispels the darkness but the presence of the dawn. Let us be so living in the acknowledgement of God's presence in us, (living in the Spirit), that when we draw near people, the light of the Kingdom dawns on them through our lives (Matthew 5:14). It is our acknowledgement of His presence in us that makes the communication of our faith effective (Philemon v.6). When they see the righteousness, peace, and joy of His Holy Spirit in us, the Kingdom of Heaven is dawning on them (Romans 14:17).

When the truth began to dawn on me, that the gospel was not a message about what God expected me to do about the sin in my life, I too began to squint at the brilliance of news, in comparison to the dullness of instruction. I imagined myself in conversations with people where they would say to me, "So you are saying that we can all just do what we want then?" and I imagined my reply as "No, I am not saying you can just do what you want." But with that reply, there always came a check in my spirit, a prompt from the Holy Spirit to pause and think again. Somehow that statement was falling short of the truth. I was becoming aware that, in fact, God does want people to do what they want. With all His heart, He wants you to do what you want. Allow me to explain.

My wife, Nicola, agreed to marry me thirty-six years ago. She knew that this decision meant she would ultimately have to leave her home in England and move to live in Ireland. Imagine if after all these years I asked her to tell me honestly why she married me and she replied that it was really because she hadn't wanted to end up living in England. She thought it would be hell compared to Ireland! In other words, she had said 'Yes' to me because she was afraid of the consequences of saying 'No.' Marrying me wasn't what her heart desired, but rather what she felt she needed to do, to avoid something worse. How do you think I would feel on hearing such an admission—that marrying me wasn't what she *really* wanted to do? Would you be surprised to hear me say, "But

I wanted you to want me. I wanted your heart. I wanted you to do what you want!"

Is God too not entitled to say to us, "I want your heart? I want you to be doing what you want to do, not what you feel you ought to do." Authentic worship is to be living the life we want to live, not the life we feel we ought to live.

Is there a way God can say to us, "You can do what you want"? Yes. He can say that when He knows that knowing Him will change our wants, that knowing Him will change our hearts. To know Him and how much He is *for* you, changes your wants, because to know Him is to find the acceptance and love that your heart was made for and is craving for in all the wrong places (Luke 15:17, 18). His Spirit, the knowing of Him, changes our wants (Romans 8:15, 16). The greatest liberty is to know such security in the love of another, that you can live no longer for yourself but for the one who loves you (2 Corinthians 5:15). This liberty is ours through knowing the love of God, poured into our hearts by God's Spirit (Romans 5:5). It is the liberty of a heart that is doing what it wants. But what it wants has been formed by the Spirit of love that has filled it, for God never made our hearts to be alone (Genesis 2:18).

God never expected us to love Him without knowing Him, no more than I would have expected Nicola to marry me without knowing me. God never expected us to believe in Him without encountering Him, and this is why He has given us His Holy Spirit. This has always been His promise: that He would never leave us to change ourselves, He would never leave us to save ourselves, as if by our willpower alone we can transform ourselves into His image (John 15:4, 5). This is why the apostle John can describe us as children not born of a mere human 'decision' but born of God (John 1:13).

It is by beholding Christ, the truth about love, that our hearts are transformed (2 Corinthians 3:18), and this has always been His plan. The Gospel has never been 'Behave!' It has always been 'Behold!' *"For God, who said, 'Let light shine out of darkness,' made his light shine in our hearts to give us the light of the knowledge of God's glory displayed in the face of Christ."*[76] (2 Corinthians 4:6).

It was never His intention to leave us to save ourselves. Listen again to that promise given through the prophet Ezekiel over 500 years before Christ came: *"I will sprinkle clean water on you, and you will be clean; I will cleanse you from all your impurities and from all your idols. I will give you a new heart and put a new spirit in you; I will remove from you your heart of stone and give you a heart of flesh. And I will put my Spirit in you and move you to follow my decrees and be careful to keep my laws. Then you will live in the land I gave your ancestors; you will be my people, and I will be your God. I will save you from all your uncleanness."*[77] (Ezekiel 36:25-29)

Can you hear what he is saying? Eight times He declares, "I!" It was never His intention that my 'I' would be left alone to try and save 'I,' but through Christ that old 'I' would be put to death and by the power of His Spirit we would each be able to say what the apostle Paul said: *"I have been crucified with Christ; it is no longer I who live, but Christ lives in me."*[78] (Galatians 2:20). It was always the Father's plan that He would never leave us to save ourselves. Jesus Christ, His life, death, resurrection, and ascension, is God not leaving us to save ourselves.

I am not ashamed to say that I have found that there is power in this gospel of *His* grace and *His* obedience (Romans 1:16). It is a power I never found in a gospel about *my* obedience. That power is the power to deliver me from myself, my self-saving life, and translate me into a life called *'hidden with Christ, in God'*[79] (Colossians 3:1-4). It is the power to rise from becoming to being, from endlessly trying to become good enough for heaven, to knowing Christ in me as my hope, my present reality (Colossians 1:27), for to know God through Christ, is to know Him as Emmanuel, God with

---

[76] New International Version.
[77] New International Version.
[78] New King James Version.
[79] New King James Version.

us (Matthew 1:23). When the Gospel dawns, it is because of the presence of God's Spirit, for again, it is not the promise of the dawn that dispels the darkness, but the presence of the dawn. Let those then who still sit in darkness see a great light, His presence in His Church. Let a great sound go forth from these children of the light, a joy inexpressible and full of glory (1 Peter 1:8). At this sound, may the very stones cry out, the hearts of men, for with the Kingdom drawing near comes the gift of repentance (Ezekiel 36:26, Luke 19:40, Luke 10:9, Acts 11:18).

Chapter Seven

A presentation of power.
The Gospel and the Spirit.

· · · ·

How many of you reading this can remember a world before the internet? Back in the day when I was at school, if you had an obscure question that needed answering for your homework, like details on a foreign country or an historical event, the only way to get that answer was to travel to your local library and look for a book on the subject. Today we can pick up our smartphone and get an answer in seconds, but before the digital age, tracking down such information was going to take you hours.

That was certainly the case for our family back in 1976, when suddenly one day the answer to all our problems appeared at our front door in the form of a traveling salesman. He claimed that he had something to sell us that would, in effect, bring the local library to us! Now he wasn't a time traveler from the future who had come to 1976 with a mobile phone, but what he did have with him was a full set of the World Book Encyclopedia. This collection of books was (according to him) nothing less than a fountain of knowledge. It would ensure that any question we children ever had, we would be able to find the answer right in our own front room.

Well, he must have been a good salesman because he got past my mom (which few salesmen ever did), and he was ushered into the front room with his large box of books.

Now in my memory, what happened next is a bit of a blur, but after all these years, two things still stand out. Firstly, this guy had us wrapped around his little finger within ten minutes because he made these books sound astonishing. He took us for a spin around the world with amazing facts, pictures, maps, and graphs. He promised that with the information these books contained, our lives were going to be transformed, especially the educational prospects of us children. He was doing such a great job at selling their value to us as a family, that it quickly became clear to me that Mum and Dad would be neglecting their duty as parents, to almost the point of criminality, if they didn't immediately purchase these books. Note to the wise here: never let your children sit in on a sales presentation! But it honestly didn't appear to us children that Mum and Dad would take much persuasion. They looked as enthralled as we were about the idea of their children being transformed into geniuses overnight.

The second thing I remember about that event, was the way the atmosphere in the room suddenly changed when the salesman was asked the inevitable question. How much will this cost us? On hearing his answer, I think my father nearly needed to be resuscitated. I can't remember the figure, but even to our young ears, we recognised this man was asking for a king's ransom. Now my mum and dad were always extremely polite people, so although I can't remember how exactly they ushered this man out, I am sure they convinced him that they would give his offer every consideration and be in touch. Unfortunately for them, the damage was done. Their children had caught a glimpse of a brave new world, and we weren't about to let Mum or Dad forget what we had seen.

In response to all our questions, we were told that Dad would soon make his decision and let us know. Now, as far as our young minds were concerned, that couldn't take long. After all, what could be difficult about a decision like that? We were about to discover that a decision is only easy, when someone else must make it. Dad turned the tables on us. He gathered us together and announced that for the same cost of those encyclopedias, we could buy a new TV—wait for it, a colour TV! So he had decided to leave the choice up to us children. Which did we want more, a set of encyclopedias or a colour TV?

Looking back on it now, I find it difficult to believe that any parent would seriously believe that their children would choose books over a new TV. The thought crossed my mind that maybe Dad had wanted a colour TV for himself all along and saw an opportunity to get us to make that decision for him. But reflecting on it, I can see now that he just wasn't good at making those sorts of decisions, because in the end he went for the option that would make the most people happy; he bought both! And so, for years the complete set of the World Book encyclopedia sat proudly on the shelf in our TV room and remained largely untouched, while we all gathered around the colour TV each night. As a testimony to how untouched the whole set was, it survived for another 45 years in my own home!

Now the reason I related that story, is that increasingly in recent years, when I have watched the way the gospel is commonly presented, I have thought of that salesman. Think of how he must have felt going from door to door, knowing that no matter how good his presentation was, no matter how much he managed to convince any family that he had good news for them, there would always come a moment where he would have to break the bad news to them: that to benefit from his good news, they were going to have to pay for it! Yes, it was good news, but not for all people, only for those who could pay the price. Yes, his product was good, but he was offering this goodness at a price.

I know now why that salesman worked so hard on his presentation. His only hope of making a sale, was in his presentation being so good that it would convince at least some people to spend what they probably didn't have to purchase it. Such a salesman then would need to be articulate, a great communicator, and someone who knew those books in enough detail to be able to convincingly answer any questions or objections people might have.

What I have just described to you, is the reason many believers feel totally inadequate to share the Gospel. We have grown up with the idea that the way that salesman made his presentation, is also the way the gospel must be presented. Tell them the good news, and then tell them the price. We could call it the "if you" message. You, too, can avail yourself of this good news, *if you* are willing to pay the price. All that God has for you can be yours *if you,* in exchange, will provide Him with what He needs from you. God's salvation, His very life, He will give to you, *if you* will first give Him *your* repentance and belief.

In other words, we present the Gospel as if repentance and belief are what God is expecting people to produce themselves, as if repentance and belief are 'of ourselves.'

But if repentance and faith were something that we could produce 'of ourselves,' then we could boast in our salvation. We could look down our noses at the world and judge them as somehow less than us, because they have not done what we did, by ourselves: repented and believed. There's only one problem, Church. We didn't repent and believe by ourselves!

Were we not saved in the same way the apostle Paul was? Listen again to how he described our salvation to the Ephesians: *"For it is by grace you have been saved, through faith—and this is not from yourselves, it is the gift of God—not by works, so that no one can boast."*[80] (Ephesians 2:8, 9) How can we leave the world with the impression that we repented and believed by ourselves, when the very faith that enabled us to do that is not of ourselves? It was given to us as the gift of His grace. (Romans 10:17).

Jesus made this clear to Nicodemus when he told him, *"That*

---

[80] New International Version.

which has been born of the flesh is flesh, and that which has been born of the Spirit is spirit."[81] (John 3:6) Listen to that same verse from the New Living Translation: *"Humans can reproduce only human life, but the Holy Spirit gives birth to spiritual life."*[82] Christian, you did nothing by yourself, because according to Jesus, apart from Him, His grace, His Spirit, we can do nothing. (John 15:5). God is not expecting people to come up with repentance and faith in Christ 'by themselves,' because 'by themselves' is the very condition that they are perishing from!

God forbid, but if you were drowning in a river and cried out for someone to save you and I came along and stood on the riverbank shouting instructions on what you needed to do to save yourself, would that have been what you had in mind when you cried out for a saviour? Do you want someone who stands back from you, shouting instructions on what you need to do to repent from drowning, or do you want someone who puts himself between you and what is killing you, someone who unites his body with yours, to save you? The good news is not that Jesus Christ is our instructor. He is our Saviour!

When that encyclopedia salesman had finished his presentation, there was nothing more he could do for us. We were left by ourselves, to come up with the resources needed ourselves to avail of what was being offered to us. For the majority of people hearing his presentation, being left 'by themselves' with no help, meant they had no choice but to decline what was being offered. That salesman's presentation was wonderful, but it had no power to change our state, our 'by ourselves' state. By the time he had finished his presentation, we were still in the same state he found us in—by ourselves—and he was looking to us and us alone for the power/resources/money to receive what he was offering. In other words, that salesman's presentation, no matter how much it first sounded like good news to us, in the end only pointed us to ourselves as our hope.

---

[81] New King James Version.
[82] New Living Translation.

That is not a description of the Gospel of Jesus Christ. The Gospel is not powerless to change our state, for indeed we are born again through the Word of God (1 Peter 1:23). In fact, in the words of the apostle Paul, the gospel " *...is the power of God unto salvation*"[83] (Romans 1:16). In the Gospel is the power to take you out of the 'by yourself' life, and into the 'with God' life, because in the Gospel itself is the power to repent and believe (Acts 11:18). That power is nothing less than the faith of Jesus Christ that comes by hearing the Gospel, (the gospel that points you to Christ as your saviour, not the one that points you to you as your saviour) (Romans 10:17). As Jesus said, *"Beware of the yeast of the Pharisees"*[84] (Matthew 16:6). Beware any presentation about God that leaves your hope on yourself, because down that road lies only despair or hypocrisy (Matthew 23:27, 28).

No matter how wonderful a presentation that salesman made, he left us as he found us: by ourselves. Now listen carefully to what I am going to say next. Christian, when we present the Gospel of Jesus Christ, there is the power present not to leave people by themselves, but to bring them into an experience of Emmanuel, God with us. That power is His very presence in our lives (John 17:20-23). That power is *His* life (Acts 9:3-5). When we stand and proclaim the Gospel, His life is present (1 Corinthians 12:3). The people we are speaking to are in the presence of God, for do we not carry the presence of God? (2 Corinthians 13:3-6). Are we not the temple of the Holy Spirit? (1 Corinthians 6:19). Are we not the very living proof before them of what we are saying? (Matthew 5:14, 15). Did Jesus not say that when you and I as believers draw near the men and women of this world, we can declare to them that the very Kingdom of God has drawn near them? (Luke 10:8, 9).

The body of Christ can proclaim what the head proclaimed, and if we look at what Jesus proclaimed, it was *"Repent, for the*

---

[83] King James Bible.
[84] New Living Translation.

Kingdom of God is at hand."[85] (Matthew 4:17). The Kingdom is His rule and reign, His presence. Can you hear what we are to proclaim to people? "Repent, for the presence of God is here!" Can you see it yet? God never expected people to repent, apart from the power of His Kingdom (1 Corinthians 2:4, 5). He doesn't separate 'Repent' from 'The Kingdom of God is at hand.' The two always go together. He never expected people to repent apart from His presence (Luke 24:15). He never expected people to repent ... by themselves, for how are people who have only known darkness to recognise darkness unless light comes? (Matthew 4:16, Acts 26:18).

In fact, Jesus' full instruction to His disciples in Luke 9 as He sent them out, was to proclaim the Kingdom of God and demonstrate it, by the power He gave them (Luke 9:1, 2). In other words, don't just tell people God has drawn near them; *be* the presence of God drawing near them! Don't stand back from people issuing them instructions on how to get out of their darkness; *be* the light that dispels their darkness! (Philippians 2:15)

God's way to bring men and women to repentance is to draw near them by His presence, for it is not possible for man to repent apart from the Spirit of God (1 Corinthians12:3). If men and women cannot repent apart from the presence of God, then can you see that Christ's purpose in bringing a Spirit-filled body, His Church, into the earth, was not so that we can shout at this world from our ivory towers to repent, but so that we can be the very presence of God living in their midst, apart from which they cannot repent? No wonder the Church is exhorted to *"be filled with the Spirit."*[86] (Ephesians 5:18), for it is as we live in the reality of the power and presence of God, that through our lives He is drawing near people by His presence (Philemon 1:6).

The more we acknowledge the abundance of His grace, His life towards us and in us, the more we are filled to overflowing with

---

[85] New King James Version.
[86] New King James Version.

the presence of God and walk as children of light (Ephesians 5:8-19). For indeed it is God Himself at work in us, and His presence causes us to shine in this world (Philippians 2:13-15). It is His presence shining out of us that causes men's eyes to open to the darkness they have been living in, for only the truth—God with us—dispels the darkness of the lie that God left us, by ourselves (2 Corinthians 4:6).

Jesus never expected people to find their way out of darkness, by themselves. He told His disciples that He would send His Holy Spirit so that people would perceive the darkness they are living in and turn to the light (John 16:7, 8). He has placed His life, His light, in us, His Church, and He now declares to us, *"You are the light of the world"*[87] (Matthew 5:14). Would He not still say to us, "Don't complain about the darkness. Let your light shine. Let my life in you and your life in me so shine with love, joy, peace, and patience … in all circumstances (1 Thessalonians 5:16-18), that people repent of not believing in Emmanuel. For in seeing you, they will be seeing Emmanuel, God with us."

In Luke 24 we are given a beautiful account of how the Lord's presence, freely given, leads men to repentance. It describes two disciples walking away from the call of God on their lives, when they meet a stranger on the road to Emmaus. They have just witnessed the crucifixion of Jesus. They are deeply disappointed and heartbroken, for they believe that the presence of God, Christ, appears to have been withdrawn from them. As they walk along trying to reason out why this has happened, Jesus joins them, and we become aware that, far from God's presence being withdrawn from them, He is actually freely giving Himself to them, even as they are walking in the wrong direction!

Earlier we saw how Jesus told His disciples to proclaim, *"Repent, for the kingdom of heaven has 'come near'."*[88] (Matthew 4:17). That

---

[87] New International Version.
[88] New International Version.

same Greek word *'engizō'*[89] is used here to describe Jesus *'drawing near'* the two disciples on the road to Emmaus.

As He draws near to them and speaks, these disciples later describe the effect as feeling their hearts burning within them.

Here is a presentation that is not leaving them in the same state! There is an awakening going on to the presence of God (Isaiah 60:1). But I want to draw your attention to the moment their eyes open. What does this passage say was happening in the moment their eyes opened? What happened to enable them to recognise Emmanuel, God with us? What caused them to have a metanoia, a repentance, a 180-degree turnaround in the direction they were going?

"Then they drew near to the village where they were going, and He indicated that He would have gone farther. But they constrained Him, saying, 'Abide with us, for it is toward evening, and the day is far spent.' And He went in to stay with them. Now it came to pass, as He sat at the table with them, that He took bread, blessed and broke it, and gave it to them. Then their eyes were opened, and they knew Him; and He vanished from their sight."[90] (Luke 24:28-31).

Can you see the progression of the presence of God being given, like the dawn rising? He draws near to them in His listening. He draws near to them in His speaking. He draws near to them in his sitting with them. He draws near to them in His giving to them. Finally, these verses declare that it was as Jesus was giving them bread to eat, that their eyes were opened. The power to repent, to have a metanoia, comes in the giving of Christ, the bread of life (John 6:35).

Listen to those verses again, that describe the moment the eyes of the disciples were opened to recognise Jesus, to see Emmanuel, God with us. *"He took the bread and blessed it, and He broke it and began giving it to them. And then their eyes were opened, and they recognized*

---

[89] Strongs Number G1448. https://www.blueletterbible.org/lexicon/g1448/kjv/tr/0-1/
[90] New King James Version.

Him."[91] In those verses we are being brought back to where mankind first fell into the darkness of unbelief. This is the very phrase used to describe what happened to Adam and Eve in the garden. Eve offered Adam the fruit of the tree of the knowledge of good and evil, and listen to what happens next from Genesis 3:6, 7. "*...she also gave some to her husband with her, and he ate. Then the eyes of both of them were opened, and they knew that they were naked; and they sewed fig leaves together and made themselves coverings.*"[92]

Is it not amazing that when Jesus gives His presence to those disciples, their eyes are opened to see Emmanuel, God with us, and they arise and run straight back to the body of Christ? But when Adam and Eve ate of the tree of the knowledge of good and evil (the self-effort tree), when they ate of the lie that God had left them to become like Him *by themselves*, their eyes could no longer see past themselves. Suddenly all they could see was that they were naked. They fell into the darkness of shame and self-consciousness. They fell from being to becoming, from communion to self-effort, and they arose and ran also. But they ran from God.

Each time we fall for the lie that we must save ourselves, we estrange ourselves from Christ (Galatians 5:4). Restoration to life in His presence does not come through our work in His fields, but in our sitting at His table (Luke 15:21-24). He takes hold of us through the proclamation of the Gospel as His presence, not just His promise, and as we will see later, this is not a matter of words but of His power present in the life of the one who brings His Gospel (1 Corinthians 2:4).

When the gospel was preached in the power of the Spirit, people didn't just find themselves with a promise from God; they found themselves in the presence of God (1 Corinthians 2:1-5). They didn't need to be motivated, for they found themselves translated,

---

[91] New International Version.
[92] New King James Version.

from the dominion of darkness into the Kingdom of the Son. They found themselves knowing communion with the Father, through the Son and by the Spirit (Colossians 1:13). Did it never strike you as remarkable that time and again throughout the New Testament, converts were baptised on the spot? Their experience was not so much one of asking Jesus into their lives, but rather finding themselves in the presence of one who was claiming their life as His own! (Acts 2:37, Acts 9:3-5).

The Gospel presented in the power of His Spirit does not leave you by yourself, because 'by yourself' is the very condition you are perishing from. The most wonderful life to live, is not the one you are chasing called 'the absence of trouble,' but the one that finds you called 'the presence of God.' To be found by the Shepherd is the turning point of our lives, but it is the Shepherd who must get the glory for that, not the lost sheep!

I have found this gospel of God's grace to be the only message that carries the power to set me free from myself and all my efforts to save myself, because it is not a message of what will be, if I first, but the declaration of what is, because He first! Every time we make the gospel a message about what could be, 'if you', we take the power from the message, because the Holy Spirit doesn't come to confirm what could be, if I. He comes to declare what *is,* because Christ! (1 Corinthians 1:17).

Now if you want to give people good advice, on things they should or shouldn't do that will help them in their faith, that is wonderful. Only please do the world a big favour; stop calling that the Gospel! Stop mixing that advice into the Gospel because the Holy Spirit witnesses to what is, not what might be, and if you keep mixing the good news with good advice, you will end up with a gospel that doesn't liberate people from themselves but brings them into a lifetime of self-effort. You will end up with a gospel that doesn't make them radiant but makes them religious, a gospel that doesn't bring them into dependency on Christ, but dependency on 'doing' church. That's a powerless gospel. To make the gospel about what men need to do, in the words of Paul, makes *"the cross of Christ be emptied of its power."*[93] (1 Corinthians 1:17).

A world that does not know of a Saviour, can only teach men how to save themselves. Such a world is flooded with advice on 'what you need to do to save yourself.' The more our 'gospel' becomes tainted with such advice, the more our churches become mere advice centres. Now, if you want to attract and keep advice consumers, then your steady supply of principles and teachings on 'what you need to do to please God' must never come to an end. Consumers must not be allowed to grow out of their fears and their need for instruction. Obviously, a gospel that declares that Christ is the end of all this self-help religion (Romans10:4) would be bad for business! Give them a lesser gospel, and they will never grow out of their fears (1 John 4:18). They will keep coming to keep hearing, what they need to keep doing in order to be saved. Unfortunately, the only message such advice consumers then carry into the world, sounds very much like "Here is what *you* need to do to save yourself". If the world doesn't appear to be listening, could it be that they have remembered what the Church forgot—the difference between good advice and good news—and that is a world of difference!

I have found that those most open to the Gospel of God's grace, are those who have been around long enough in the fields of religion, to have lost all confidence in their own ability to lead a holy life (1 Timothy 1:15, 16).

To present the Gospel in power, is not to offer a set of books full of wisdom, as a means to attaining to righteousness, holiness, and redemption, for it is not to present *a* way of salvation, but *the* way of salvation: Christ. It is to present Him *"who has become for us wisdom from God—that is, our righteousness, holiness, and redemption"*[94] (1 Corinthians 1:30), for faith cannot rest in what might be, but only in what is!

---

[93] New International Version.
[94] New International Version.

The Gospel is not the promise of what might be, if I live well or die well. It is the proclamation of what is, because of Christ's life and death. This is how the early church overcame the might of the Roman Empire. Those rulers of the ancient world could only watch dumbfounded as countless Christians went to their deaths singing, because their hope had been established in what is, not in what might be.

Chapter Eight

Perplexed by the Gospel.

····

I recently heard an account of a father in India who had watched his daughter over many months descend into the darkness of a life of addiction to drugs. He saw everything precious slowly taken from her: her body disfigured and destroyed, her dignity and her relationships broken, and finally, with all hope gone, her inevitable death. In witnessing the horror of it all, her father at one point cried out that he would gladly swap places with her and take all her pain and suffering and humiliation, if only she could have his life and live free from this curse.

If we do not hear in that cry, the depth of the love that our heavenly father has for all people, the love of a father who could not stand to see our lives disfigured by sin and death, then we will never grasp just how serious God was about entering into the full darkness of our separation, that we might know the full light of union with the Godhead (Matthew 27:46, Luke 22:44, Romans 8:16, 17, Colossians 1:13, 2 Peter 1:4). On the day of Pentecost, the message that first drew the church out of the building it was hiding in, was not about meeting God in heaven one day, *if* we ... It was the revelation that He is here. He came. God is with us, today!

When the extravagance of the gospel of God's grace began to dawn on me, I began to realise that this message about Christ was not a religion for the pious, but a gospel for the powerless. It was not a message about what life could be like, one day in the by-and-by, but about a life that could be experienced today. The implications of this were unsettling. It was as if I had been living all my life waiting for a verdict that had already been delivered. I had thought that life with God would begin in heaven one day, *if* my life passed God's inspection. I lived under the shadow of that huge 'if.'

But what if the life inspected was not my imperfect life, but Christ's perfect life? What if the lamb that takes away the sin of the world had already been inspected? (John 1:29). What if heaven couldn't wait, because Love couldn't wait to be with us (John 3:16). This gospel of Jesus Christ was claiming that God had already done, what all my life I had understood religion to be telling me was my job! Apparently, He had (without my permission) reconciled me (and the whole world) to Himself and was now no longer counting our sins against us! (2 Corinthians 5:19). I struggled with the extravagance of such a message. I simply wasn't used to a gospel that didn't involve me playing a starring role in doing something about my own sins! You could say I was perplexed.

I know this now to be a good sign, a sign that I was hearing the gospel correctly, for earthly religion sounds eminently reasonable in comparison to the scandalous gospel of God's grace (Acts 10:17, Romans 10:1-4, 1 Corinthians 1:21, Galatians 1:11). Struggling with contradiction, is often the cradle for revelation. We grow in the knowledge of God as we face up to the question of how God can be perfectly good and yet the world be in such a state. Far from shying away from such questions, the New Testament records Jesus asking three times more questions than He was asked Himself. He used such questions to challenge deeply rooted mindsets that had left man constantly looking to himself for hope. If you are reading this book and have no questions about how God can be good and the world so broken, just hang on a few years. You soon will have! (John 16:33).

Acts 10:17 tells us that when the Holy Spirit began to open the apostle Peter's understanding to the extravagance and generosity of God, he was greatly perplexed. The Greek word used to describe his mental state, '*diaporeō*' means to be '*in doubt*' '*to be much perplexed*'[95] The Lord knew that in sending the apostle Peter to preach the gospel to Gentiles (non-Jews) in a Roman household for the first time, he would find it very difficult to see past the fact that they were not Jews. The temptation for Peter to mix some instruction in with the gospel, on how to make yourself more acceptable to God (you must do what we do), would have been overwhelming. Grace sounds offensive to our religious sensibilities, as we think it quite reasonable that God should first require us to clean our act up, to make ourselves worthy enough to be saved. Religion (self-effort) always makes more sense to the natural man, for his hope has always been in himself.

To speak words of the Spirit, we must be seeing people according to the Spirit, for how we see determines how we speak (2 Corinthians 5:16). The more we see people merely by their earthly record, the more we can't resist expressing the gospel as instruction: 'This is what you need to do!" The Lord had to therefore prepare Peter by giving him a revelation of how even these non-Jews looked to God in the light of Christ's finished work. This came in the form of a vision in which Peter was instructed to eat animals that every Jew believed to be 'unclean' (Acts 10:9-14). God was, in effect, changing Peter's view, his vision, on what was clean to God and what was unclean. He did this by declaring something to him three times. "*Do not call anything impure that God has made clean.*"[96] (Acts 10:15).

Why did Peter need such supernatural admonition, and not just once but repeatedly? I believe it was because his understanding of the Gospel was still being 'unveiled' because of his reverence

---

[95] Strongs Number G1280. https://www.blueletterbible.org/lexicon/g1280/kjv/tr/0-1/
[96] Berean Standard Bible.

for the Mosaic Law (Matthew 17:4, 5). This unveiling was spoken of by the apostle Paul in his second letter to the Corinthians (2 Corinthians 3:7-18). Jesus Himself had also spoken to Peter and the other disciples of truths that they were not yet able to bear, but that would be revealed by the Holy Spirit at the proper time (John 16:12, 13). What was being 'unveiled' to Peter was that the glory of the gospel is not found in the bringing of condemnation (as the Law did), but in the bringing of righteousness (2 Corinthians 3:9). The Law revealed the glory that was missing from our lives, but the Gospel is the dawning of the glory of God rising on our lives (Isaiah 60:1-3).

Without a revelation of the surpassing glory of the New Covenant over the Old, it was inevitable that Peter would mix in a little law with the gospel (Matthew 17:4, 5). He would be so fixated on the uncleanness of these people according to the Law, that there was a great danger that he wouldn't be able to resist mixing in a little advice with his gospel. He would want to help these 'dirty' gentiles to first get themselves cleaned up a bit, so that they would be more worthy of inclusion in the Kingdom. Like the elder brother in Luke 15, Peter's own record of faithfulness to 'the rules' could cause him to stand back from giving these non-Jews the full welcome into the kingdom of the message of grace. How deeply this 'religious' mindset was ingrained in Peter can be seen in the fact that several years later he did exactly that. In Antioch he took a step back from gentile believers, and the apostle Paul rebuked him for it, for he understood that to step back from grace, is to step back from the Gospel! (Galatians 2:11-14).

In declaring to Peter, "*What God has cleansed, no longer consider unholy.*"[97] the Lord was saying in effect, "Don't go to these non-Jews with a message about how unclean they are. Go and tell them what I have done about their uncleanness! Don't make the gospel about what they must do for me. Give them the good announcement, the

---

[97] New American Standard Bible.

'*euangelion*' the news of what I have done for them. Declare to them that the forgiveness of sins has been given, not based on their lives, but on Christ's. Declare this to them that they may believe and receive what has been freely given, and so find themselves reconciled to God (2 Corinthians 5:18-21)."

The apostle Peter became greatly perplexed at what the Holy Spirit was showing him because he really thought that he knew the gospel. After all, had he not walked with Jesus for three years and been filled with the Holy Spirit on the day of Pentecost? Had he not seen three thousand Jews come to believe in Christ after he preached on that great day? (Acts 2:41). Yet before the Lord can send him to preach the gospel to a gathering of non-Jews, He must address a fundamental flaw in Peter's understanding. Don't you love Peter's heart? The Lord did. Here was a man who time and again blundered his way forward and yet went on to leave a great legacy because he remained humble enough to be teachable (2 Peter 3:17,18).

I believe this account of the gospel transcending one of that society's greatest barriers, the dividing wall between Jew and Gentile, holds profound truths that are relevant for all of us today who want to see the gospel overflow the banks of our religious structures and mindsets. At this pivotal moment for the spread of the gospel across the ancient world, it was not the eloquence of Peter's message that brought such a spiritual breakthrough. He was simply a man who was both carrying the presence of God's Spirit and being carried along by God's Spirit, to a degree that compelled him to do and say things that ran counter to his natural experience and thinking (2Peter1:21).

The great danger each generation of the Church faces, is that the more experience we gain in 'doing' church, the more professional we become in doing it. But the book of Acts is not an account of the exploits of experienced professionals but anointed amateurs! They weren't trying to make or preserve the reputation of a church but were simply allowing the love of God to compel them to speak of

Him (2Corinthians 5:14,15). There is no such thing as a 'successful' Christian, any more than there is such a thing as a 'successful' toddler. Both are utterly dependent on the life of another (John 15:4,5).

As Peter arrives at the house of someone he has never imagined visiting, he finds himself in a state of awe. He is amazed at how far out of the boat the voice of the Lord has called him to walk this time! (Acts 10:28). He still can't quite believe what God has shown him about the efficacy of Christ's death and resurrection for anyone who will believe, even non-Jews. As he enters the home of this Roman centurion, Peter expresses his incredulity to Cornelius by saying something that he knows would not be acceptable to say in the church in Jerusalem. But by the Spirit it is possible to say things we cannot say by our natural understanding (1Cor.2:13,14). Peter hears himself say these words; *"God has shown me that I should not call any man common or unclean."*[98] (Acts 10:28). He didn't just say these words in the presence of Gentiles but also the Church, for Peter had not made this journey to Cornelius' house alone. He was accompanied by some of the believers from Joppa (Acts 10:23).

It is significant that on this crucial day for the spread of the gospel, Peter was accompanied by circumcised believers (Jewish Christians). At that time, they were the only sort of Christian there was! None of them had crossed the threshold of a Gentile house with the gospel before. Peter was being carried forward by a call of the Holy Spirit (2Peter.1:21), but his fellow believers were about to follow him across a spiritual Rubicon on the strength of their love and respect for him. Love is patient and such patience and faith will always be required to see the Gospel bear fruit on new ground (2Cor.12:12). The Lord is not in the business of raising up lone superstars but a body, and that body cannot grow beyond the love they have one for another (Ephesians 4:15,16). In the end we must

---

[98] New King James Version.

be able to say, *"It seemed good to the Holy Spirit and to us"*[99] not 'the Holy Spirit and me'! (Acts 15:28).

Peter begins to share the Gospel with those gathered, but he doesn't get very far. Within minutes all those 'unclean' gentiles are being gloriously filled with the Holy Spirit and speaking in tongues, just as Peter himself and the other disciples were on the day of Pentecost. Now listen to the words that Peter was speaking at the very moment the Holy Spirit came upon all who were listening. He was declaring that forgiveness of sins, reconciliation to God, is not given on the basis of our lives (Jew or Gentile), but Christ's. *"All the prophets testify about him that everyone who believes in him receives forgiveness of sins through his name". While Peter was still speaking these words, the Holy Spirit came on all who heard the message. The circumcised believers who had come with Peter were astonished that the gift of the Holy Spirit had been poured out even on Gentiles. For they heard them speaking in tongues and praising God.*[100] (Acts 10:43-46). Those 'circumcised believers' were the Church of that day, and they were astonished at whom God was willing to give Himself to. So astonished, that it is obvious they could not have changed their theology apart from that demonstration of power by the Holy Spirit.

For the gospel to impact nations and people groups in our generation that we cannot yet imagine reaching, we too as the Church need to have the depths of the love of God for the 'unclean' unveiled to us afresh, and our thinking perplexed! For centuries we have struggled to police the grace of God with our theological definitions of who 'qualifies' and who doesn't. But we just can't seem to find a religious box that can contain a God who qualifies us himself and the inexpressible joy that brings (Colossians 1:12, 1Peter.1:8). In the end we cannot control the wind of God's Spirit, but like Peter, we must allow ourselves to be carried along to places and people beyond our imagination (2Peter.1:21).

---

[99] New King James Version.
[100] New International Version.

Through this encounter with God's Spirit, Peter was receiving a revelation of how God saw people; not according to *their* earthly record, but according to *His* eternal purpose and grace given in Christ (2Corinthians.5:16, 2Timothy.1:9). Paul later expressed this revelation to the Corinthians in these words; *"that God was reconciling the world to himself in Christ, not counting people's sins against them. And he has committed to us the message of reconciliation."*[101] (2Corinthians.5:19). In other words, God is not asking people to become reconciled to Him by what they do or don't do, but to be reconciled to Him by accepting the reconciliation that He has provided; Christ, our *"righteousness and sanctification and redemption"*[102] (1Corinthians.1:30,31). In that sense God was telling Peter not to speak to people as if they were unclean in God's eyes (as if Christ's work of reconciliation did not encompass them). He was asking and empowering Peter to speak to them not after the flesh (according to their natural condition), but after the Spirit (according to what Christ had done for them) (2Corinthians.5:14-17) for reconciliation is not a work to be achieved, but a work to be believed (John 20:27,28).

This was a step beyond where Peter had ever gone before in his understanding of the scope of the gospel and for the circumcised believers in Jerusalem it was a step too far. Their understanding had not yet emerged from under the long shadow of the Law and in the words of Paul to the Corinthians, their hearts were 'veiled' and so their minds dulled to the full glory of the Gospel (2Corinthians.3:7-18). When news reached them that Peter had *"entered the home of Gentiles and even ate with them!"*[103] they criticised him (Acts 11:2,3). To this day in each generation, the gospel only breaks out of the religious ghettos we limit it to when the Holy Spirit shows up and challenges our theology. This can be a difficult journey.

---

[101] New International Version.
[102] New American Standard Bible.
[103] New Living Translation.

On seeing the gentiles that day being filled with God's Spirit, Peter now knew beyond any doubt that these people were accepted by God and had no problem in immediately giving them the public sign of their belonging to God, of their being born of His Spirit; he baptised them. On being challenged about his actions back in Jerusalem, his defence was simple; *"If God gave them the same gift he gave us who believed in the Lord Jesus Christ, who was I to think that I could stand in God's way?"*[104] (Acts 11:17).

It is important to note something about the immediate response of the other apostles to Peter's testimony recorded in Acts 11:18. *"When they heard these things they became silent; and they glorified God, saying, "Then God has also granted to the Gentiles repentance to life."*[105] Here the Church is having to acknowledge that God has gifted His Spirit and so the capacity to repent and believe (1Corinthians.12:3) to people they had deemed unworthy of such grace. This was the Church squinting (and not for the last time) at the brilliance of the gospel of God's grace. In their understanding they were beginning a journey, out of the shadows and into the Son. The children of light were slowly and tentatively discovering their freedom from the law of sin and death, like butterflies breaking out of their chrysalis. But that 'unveiling' of hearts would prove to be a continuing struggle (2Corinthians.3:14-17, Galatians 1:6,7, Galatians 3:1-3).

Here is the great challenge still facing the Church of each generation. How subtly our church culture of good works and service to God can move *our* life for God to centre stage in the story of our salvation, rather than *His* life for us. Is it possible to slip from Christ-life to church-life? Having begun in the Spirit as those *'granted repentance unto life"*[106] (Acts 11:18), are multitudes of us also now trying to be made perfect by our 'Christianity' (Galatians 3:3). How far have we drifted from the truth that we were powerless

---

[104] New International Version.
[105] New King James Version.
[106] King James Bible.

to save ourselves and that even our repentance unto life was the gift of His grace which came to us through the Gospel? To what extent is it time for this generation of the Church to be challenged with the same question the apostle Paul put to the Corinthians? *"For who considers you as superior? What do you have that you did not receive? And if you did receive it, why do you boast as if you had not received it?"*[107] (1Corinthians.4:7) Perhaps we can note this drift by how much the gospel of His grace, once so sweet to the ears of an amateur, now sounds too simple and even irresponsible to our professional Christian ears and so must be quarantined within a hedge of required behaviours. After all, God forbid that we would baptise someone on the spot!

To come back to Peter's defence of his actions, he simply pointed out that if God had accepted these people, how could he not do likewise? To Peter, the sign of God's acceptance was the giving of His Holy Spirit in like manner to the day of Pentecost. Acts 11 shows us that such a dramatic sign was indeed needed, to assure the early Church that Peter's apparent departure from their understanding of God's will was in fact the leading of the Holy Spirit. As Jesus had promised. *"I have many more things to say to you, but you cannot bear them at the present time. But when He, the Spirit of truth, comes, He will guide you into all the truth ..."*[108] (John 16:12,13).

This doesn't mean that the lack of such dramatic signs every time the Gospel is proclaimed today indicates any lack of acceptance by God of the hearers. But what we can miss in this account of the breakout of the Gospel into a new people group, is that the Holy Spirit first had to do a work in the one preaching the Gospel. Without that fresh anointing of the Spirit that came on that rooftop in Joppa, it is likely Peter would have approached a group of 'unclean' Gentiles with a message more about what they needed to do to be

---

[107] New American Standard Bible.
[108] New American Standard Bible.

accepted by God, rather than speak to them of God's acceptance of them through Christ.

Perhaps here too we can see the real need of each generation of the Church for a fresh baptism in the love of God; that as ministers of reconciliation we would be so cut to the heart concerning our self-righteousness, that the message of reconciliation would once again be carried as news not instruction, for news crosses boundaries that instruction cannot (Luke 2:10). The only message that can bring great joy to all people is the one that addresses the need of all people. A gospel for the clean cannot do this, but a gospel for the powerless can!

Chapter Nine

Honey, we shrunk the Gospel!

• • • •

My father's work schedule may have been hectic, but that didn't mean that he wasn't a daily presence in the lives of his children. It helped that for many years our home was also his office and surgery. Attached to the side of our house were a waiting room, a consulting room, and a small operating theatre. Dad held an evening surgery for his "small animal" clients, and people arriving at our front door with dogs and cats would be sent "around the side." People with emergencies could turn up on any day of the year, at any hour of the day or night, even on Christmas Day! In addition to all the domestic pet clients, farmers could arrive in the lambing season with sheep needing a caesarean, or we could look out the kitchen window and see a horse standing in our garden waiting for an x-ray!

It was no great surprise some evenings to find Dad so tired that he could not face another person coming to the door. Yet he never turned anyone away. Perhaps that's because on the one occasion when he tried, it didn't go too well! One evening on a particularly busy day, he had just sat down to his tea when another farmer rang the front doorbell. In exasperation he made the mistake of telling one of my sisters to go and tell this man that he wasn't at home. My sister was still at primary school and had rarely been entrusted with such an important task as to speak to a farmer on behalf of her father. Drawing herself up to her full height, she proudly opened the front door and with great gravitas, made an announcement that we still talk about to this day. "My dad says to tell you that he is not at home!" Fortunately, rather than take this as an insult, the farmer was greatly amused. The innocence of a child has the power to disarm the most hardened cynics.

Have you ever thought of God as having the innocence of a young child? Jesus was wiser than any man that ever lived, but He was also the personification of innocence. He was never self-seeking or rude or held anything against anyone He spoke to (1 Corinthians 13:5). We have a saying locally about people who appear to be vulnerable to the deception of others. We say, "He is too innocent for this world."

But Jesus' innocence was not naivety. He knew better than anyone the deception and selfishness that had taken root in the hearts of men (John 2:25). Yet He continued to speak to all people with an innocence that could disarm the hardest of hearts (Luke 19:5, John 4:17, 18). As the opposition to Him from the religious authorities grew, His disciples must have increasingly feared for His life. He must have seemed to them "too innocent for this world." Yet He refused to 'tone down' for his own good. What His disciples couldn't grasp was that He wasn't living for His own good. He had come to die for ours! (Matthew 16:21-23). Long before His disciples could fully understand His teachings or His purpose, they believed in Him. They had simply never heard another human being speak like Him (John 7:46). He was thoroughly good, and His words were life-giving (John 6:68). They had never been in the presence of such a generous soul.

I have a feeling that in our communications age, with our ready access to all the information in the world, we have forgotten the transforming power of simply being in the presence of goodness. I suspect I have spent years trying to preach people I have spent too little time with, into the knowledge of a God I have spent too little time with!

It is significant that Acts chapter two does not finish with a summary of the theology of the early church, but with a vivid description of their fellowship. In being filled with the Spirit of God, they found within themselves the generosity of God and began to share life with each other to a depth never seen before (Acts 2:44-47). Their goodness shone like a light, and day by day more people were drawn to that light (Matthew 5:14, Philippians 2:15). In an era where our concept of 'church' has increasingly come to refer to an event we attend for several hours a week whose main goal appears to be numerical growth, are we not in danger of losing the early church's greatest evangelistic witness: the depth of their fellowship! (John 13:35, 1 Corinthians 13:1-3).

By now you will have noticed that in each chapter I am repeatedly speaking of the generosity of God. This is because to encounter God in spirit and in truth is to see His goodness. When Moses cried out to God that he desired to know Him, listen to God's reply. *"And the Lord said, "I will cause all my goodness to pass in front of you ..."*[109] (Exodus 33:19) This is why I keep coming back to Jesus' parable of the prodigal son in Luke 15. It is a story of two sons who never really knew their father, until they got to see the extravagance of his giving (Luke 15:23, 31).

I wonder how true that could be of me today. I think I know what the gospel is, but in truth I have yet to discover the true extravagance of the gift given to me, and so I have yet to know the true generosity of the giver. For much of my life, I thought in the gift of the Bible the Father was saying to me, "If you obey all these commands, then one day you will be ready to receive my gift of eternal life." Whereas in truth, this gospel is not about what I could get one day in the future, if I love God enough. Rather, it is the

---

[109] New International Version.

announcement of what has already been given to me, because God loved me enough! (1 John 4:19).

Can you see then that any gospel that does not reveal just how much was given to us in the giving of Christ, cannot bring us to know Father God in the way He wants to be known? It is my conviction that in much of the Church, the way we preach the gospel does not reveal the true extravagance of the Father. The tragedy of that is that our lives cannot outgrow our beliefs (Proverbs 4:23). Spirit gives birth to spirit. People who believe in a small god live small lives. No wonder God's first commandment to Moses warned of the danger of worshipping anything or anyone that fell short of the truth of who He is (Exodus 20:3). This commandment is not the dictate of an insecure king but the concern of a loving father.

Have you noticed that the lives of believers cannot surpass their revelation of the Father? Christians who are judgmental, quick to condemn, and apparently always angry at the world, are like that because in their hearts that is what they believe God to be like, and you cannot live beyond the borders of what you have believed (Proverbs 4:23). The mouth will speak what the heart is full of (Matthew 12:34, 35). If we are living small, self-absorbed, self-conscious, fearful lives, then the root of that is what we have believed. A small gospel produces a small life.

There was a film that came out 30 years ago, about a scientist who invented a machine that could shrink things. He ended up accidentally shrinking his kids. Everything you needed to know about the film was in the title. It was called "Honey, I Shrunk the Kids." It was so successful that a few years later they brought out a sequel called "Honey, I Blew Up the kids". The sad thing is, as parents, we do have the power to shrink our kids. My fears, my anxieties, my beliefs, and my unbelief have profoundly shaped the lives of my children, for my words have shaped them, and those words were born from my beliefs. Nowhere is that more significant in their lives, than the effect on them of what I have believed about God. My beliefs became their beliefs, through the words I spoke over them (Deuteronomy 6:6, 7). In the same way flesh gave birth to flesh, spirit gave birth to spirit (John 3:6). That is what Paul meant when he said to the Corinthians, *"I became your father through the gospel."*[110] (1 Corinthians 4:15)

It is my conviction that the Gospel is much bigger, more glorious, more generous, and more joyful than we have ever known, because the lives we were destined to live in Christ have got to be bigger, more glorious, more generous, and more joyful than the small lives limited by anxiety that multitudes of us as believers are living today. Let me say that differently. If believers are living shrunken lives, it is for one reason and one reason only. Honey, we shrunk the gospel! And when you shrink the gospel, you shrink the kids.

If the gospel you are sitting under isn't revealing the enormity of what God has done in the giving of His only son, then there is no power in that gospel to bring about the transformation of your life, from someone who has been religiously self-absorbed, to someone who lives like a star-struck lover. To live life in all its abundance is to live totally smitten and transformed by the love of another (1 John 4:10). To live in such awareness of the love of God, is to find your life full of love, joy, peace, patience, kindness, goodness, faithfulness, gentleness, and self-control, for this is the fruit that grows in any life into whom the Holy Spirit is pouring the love of God (Romans 5:5, Galatians 5:22, 23).

If the gospel you are hearing isn't revealing to you the enormity of what has been freely given to you in Christ, then it will not have the power to lift you out of yourself, your self-centredness. The New Testament doesn't say that the Spirit has come from God that we may know what we need to give Him, but rather, *"that we may know the things freely given to us by God."*[111] (1 Corinthians 2:12). Which do you think has more power to free you from self-effort: a message

---

[110] New International Version.
[111] New American Standard Bible.

about what God requires of you or a message about what God has done for you?

For many years I thought the Holy Spirit was given, to teach me what to do. I thought He was as obsessed with my behaviour as I was! But it turns out that it wasn't God who thought that all I needed was to know more about good and evil, so I could try and become like him by behaving better. I wasn't created to produce life, but to partake of life. The Holy Spirit is given that we would grow in the knowledge of the Father through the Son, for to be filled with such knowledge of God is to know whose we are and what we already have in God our Father. When we know how blessed we are, we won't need anyone to tell us what to do, because we will already be doing it! (Ezekiel 36:26, 27). That's because the faith that comes from God can't help expressing itself through love (Galatians 5:22), in the same way that someone in love doesn't need instruction on how to kiss. You just can't help doing it!

Paul called the gospel 'the power of God' because the gospel He preached revealed God as He really is. Do you know God is so good that you can't know Him for who He really is and remain the same? In fact, knowing Him was always God's way of transforming our lives. As Jesus said, *"you shall know the truth, and the truth shall make you free"*[112] (John 8:32). But the truth is not a list of instructions; it is the person of God Himself (John 14:6). The power to be transformed comes from beholding Christ, not beholding instructions (2 Corinthians 3:18). Once again, being pointed to yourself can never set you free from yourself. You needed a Saviour to set you free, and you are not that Saviour.

That's why Paul was so furious when he heard that someone had come along to the Galatians and added to the gospel, because he knew that to add to the gospel, is to shrink the gospel (Galatians 1:6-9). Some religious men had come in among the Galatians and taken the pure message about God and His love, (what Paul called the

---

[112] New King James Version.

message of Christ and Him crucified) and added a little instruction to it about being circumcised. That little contamination (what Paul called 'leaven') changed the whole nature of the Gospel (Galatians 1:7). A message about God and His gift, had been reduced to one about you and your work. That little addition took the power out of the message, because being told what you need to do never set anyone free. It was a lie when it was told to Adam in the garden, and it was still a lie when it was told to the Galatians. Being pointed to yourself will never set you free from yourself. It will only turn you in on yourself more, which is why the apostle Paul declared, *"The power of sin is the Law"*[113] (1 Corinthians 15:56). The end of that self-absorbed road is either despair or hypocrisy, or a mix of both!

Such a mixture was the experience of a certain rich young ruler. He came to Jesus claiming that he had been keeping all the laws, yet he still knew that his obedience wasn't giving him eternal life (Matthew 19:16-22). He thought that the reason must be that God required more obedience. We can see this in his question to Jesus, which reveals a belief about salvation that centres around his own efforts: *"what good thing shall I do that I may have eternal life?"*[114] (Matthew 19:16). It is interesting that Jesus initially points him back to the Law, as if He knows that there is still something this young man has not realized; that he cannot keep the Law, that he cannot be like God through self-effort. This young man thinks that he needs to be stronger for God. He thinks, 'I need to do more for God.' But a stronger 'I' is not his solution; a stronger 'I' is his problem!

Stronger individuals are a problem for the whole world. Perhaps that is why the Cross looks like an I with a stroke through it. We really don't need stronger individuals; we need stronger relationships. Jesus didn't say that the world would know His disciples by their individual strength but by their love for one another, a love that looks to serve the other.

---

[113] New International version.

[114] New King James Version.

None of us were made to live independent of God's grace, His empowering presence. This young ruler needed to get to the end of 'I', his reliance on his own resources, and simply depend on the grace of God, the God-given life, Christ. The Law has led him to Christ, (the end of the Law and the end of him 'self'). At this place he finds Jesus inviting him out of separation and into relationship. This is why Jesus tells him to divest himself of his earthly resources (his ability to be his own saviour) and to receive Jesus as his provider. But this man is not ready yet to lose his 'self-life', to yield the throne of his life to another king and so he leaves in great sadness (Matthew 19:21, 22). It is never God that leaves us sad and empty, but our own pride (Luke 15:28, 29).

Everywhere in every generation, whenever the church has added a little instruction to the gospel, they have reduced a supernatural message to a natural one, for it seems eminently reasonable to the natural man that he should play some starring role in his own salvation! Only the truth can carry the power of the Spirit, and the truth is that you cannot set yourself free from sin and death by what you do for God. If you could, you wouldn't need a Saviour. That's what Paul meant when he warned the Galatians that a mixed gospel, (God does His part, and I will do mine) is no gospel at all (Galatians 1:7). To believe in yourself, is to estrange yourself from Christ and to fall from grace (Galatians 5:4). To fall from grace, is to turn your back on the power of God and go back to self-effort. No wonder the rich young ruler went away sad, for the burden of being your own saviour is too much for any man to bear. That's not living; that is only surviving, and apart from Christ, you are only surviving on death row!

Chapter Ten

The authority of intimacy: Living from union in a world of separation.

• • • •

One of the reasons my father had told his doctor that he loved his work was because being a veterinary surgeon brought him into contact with so many people from all backgrounds, and he loved meeting some great characters. He loved the 'craic' (for American readers, this is not a drug, but an Irish term for the joy of life found when folk get together!). On one occasion on his rounds, he stopped to give a lift to an old farmer he knew. This man could certainly have been described as a well-known local 'character'. His life had had been in turmoil for years, as the poor man was an alcoholic and had drunk away all his possessions. He had literally liquidated all his assets! That morning, he told my father that he was on his way to a doctor's appointment and proceeded to tell the story of what happened at his last visit. As he had been suffering with a sore throat, the doctor decided to look down the back of his throat with a laryngoscope (a medical instrument with a light and a lens, used to visualize the voice-box). After a thorough examination, the doctor announced, "Good news. I can see nothing." The response of the farmer was not what he expected. "What do you mean you can see nothing? I have poured thirty acres of land, forty cattle, and two tractors down there, and you can see nothing!"

We all have an insatiable thirst for life, for we were made for nothing less than communion with God. It was Jesus who said to the Samaritan woman at the well, *"Whoever drinks of this water will thirst again, but whoever drinks of the water that I shall give him will never thirst. But the water that I shall give him will become in him a fountain of water springing up into everlasting life."*[115] (John 4:13.14). Notice Jesus did not ask this woman to produce anything, only to partake of what he was giving. Jesus is the life-giver, not the life-demander, and He told His disciples, *"The words that I speak to you are spirit, and they are life."*[116] (John 6:63).

Of all the people who ever walked the earth, the person who said the most extraordinary words that have ever been uttered, was Jesus Christ. Who else had ever said to a man who had been dead for four days, *"Come forth!"*[117] (John 11:43) Who else had ever said to a cripple, *"Your sins are forgiven you"*[118] (Matthew 9:2) and then *"Get up, pick up your stretcher and go home."*[119] (Matthew 9:6). Who else has ever said of Himself, *"Destroy this temple, and I will raise it again in three days"?*[120] (John 2:19). Yet on being asked about the things He said, the apostle John records Jesus' amazing answer. He said of His own words, *"I did not speak on my own, but the Father who sent me commanded me to say all that I have spoken. ... Whatever I say, is just what the Father has told me to say!"*[121] (John 12:49,50).

According to Jesus, He spoke the most extraordinary words ever uttered, because He was hearing the most extraordinary words ever

---

[115] New King James Version.
[116] New King James Version.
[117] King James Bible.
[118] New King James Version.
[119] New American Standard Bible.
[120] New International Version.
[121] New International Version.

uttered! His was a life in conversation and in communion with His father, in the power of the Spirit. His quality of life was never a life lived for himself, but a life shared.

This is the life we receive in Christ, for in Him we were raised as one body, not a multitude of like-minded individuals. *"There is one body and one Spirit, just as you were called to one hope when you were called; one Lord, one faith, one baptism; one God and Father of all, who is over all and through all and in all."*[122] (Ephesians 4:4-6) Just as it would be strange for me to talk to my wife about 'my' children, so must it sound strange for the heavenly realm to hear Christians speak of 'my' faith and 'my' life for God, when in truth the life we have been gifted in Christ, is 'our' life from God.

Salvation is to receive and live from the life that He has given. It is to find our true life as birthed from His, or in the words of Jesus to Nicodemus, *"born of the Spirit"*[123] (John 3:8). On being asked by Nicodemus how this comes about, listen to Jesus' response and note the distinct absence of any instruction! *"The wind blows wherever it pleases. You hear its sound, but you cannot tell where it comes from or where it is going. So it is with everyone born of the Spirit."*[124] (John 3:8).

Notice that Jesus never points Nicodemus to himself, but to the ministry of God's Spirit. The gospel is more than mere instruction; it is the impartation of the power of God, for as our eyes are lifted to behold the love of the Father in the face of Christ, we see His is a love that does not demand righteousness but supplies it. (Romans 1:16, 17). His is a love that so loves us, that He gives all (John 3:16). We have no business preaching the gospel as if it is mere information, an earthly sales pitch. If we cannot speak ourselves as those humbled and overwhelmed by the presence of God, as those scarcely believing we have been given the privilege of speaking such

---

[122] New International Version.

[123] New International Version.

[124] New International Version.

things (1 Corinthians 2:1-10), then let us stay silent, for flesh only gives birth to flesh (John 3:6).

To preach the gospel in the power of the Spirit is not to present people with the promise of God but the very presence of God, for we have not been given the Spirit that we would merely preach an earthly message more eloquently (1 Corinthians 2:4). Even if the Church has forgotten, the Holy Spirit still knows that it was not an earthly message about getting to heaven one day, that caused the Church to first break out of the building it had locked itself in (Acts 2:3, 4). It was the glorious, unearthly, foolish message that can only be known by the Spirit: that we have been given something better than heaven one day. "Look! Behold! Today we have the King of Heaven living in us!". Only when the Church becomes intoxicated again with the reality that we are now the dwelling place of God, will she rise to despise death and trumpet the sufficiency of Christ's life, death, and resurrection (Hebrews 2:14, 15).

This is why it is significant that in Jesus' parable of the prodigal son, the father does not just speak to the son; he physically imparts to him what he has (Luke 15:22, 23). The gospel is not just a matter of words, an intellectual proposition to be reasoned with. It is the empowerment of God to partake of His life (1 Corinthians 2:1-5). It is a pouring out of the speaker and a pouring into the hearer of the life, the Spirit of God. For this reason, the power of the gospel is not just found in the choice of words or eloquence of delivery, but in the power of the communion of spirit that the speaker is living in with God's Spirit (1 Corinthians 2:1-5, 1 Corinthians 6:17, Acts 2:1-4, Acts 4:13). It is not just a matter of what is being said, but who is saying it.

The authority given to us in Christ is never something separate from God's Spirit but is in essence our intimacy with Him. We carry authority to the extent that we are under authority, for the only words that carry the authority of the Kingdom are those proceeding from the King. In a world that did not know of such intimacy with God, people assumed Jesus was speaking as an individual. It took a

Roman soldier to recognise that Jesus spoke with authority because He was living as someone under authority, someone submitted to the will of another (Matthew 8:8, 9). This is why, on being asked about His supernatural works, Jesus always spoke in terms of what He could see the Father doing (John 5:19-20) or hear the Father saying (John 12:49, 50).

Still today, for the Gospel to break out of the respectable religious structures we have built around it and break into new people groups, we need to be being filled with the Holy Spirit (Ephesians 5:18). Contrary to popular evangelical culture, this is less to do with harsh treatment of the body and more to do with hearing the Gospel again in all its radical purity, for it is the only message that can set us free from ourselves and our religion! (Galatians 2:11-21). Any message that says, in effect, "Here is what you need to do, in order to become" is an earthly message, for it is pointing you to yourself as your own saviour. Remember, all a world that doesn't know the Saviour can do, is teach you to be your own!

No matter how many Bible verses are quoted to try and justify it, the message "Try harder to be holier" is an earthly message, because there is no heavenly power in any message that points you to yourself. The Law's good purpose was to reveal our inability to be as God is, that we would get to the end of all our efforts to be righteous, and in coming to the end of ourselves, we would come to Christ, the end of the Law for righteousness and the gift of God's righteousness. (Romans 3:19, Romans 10:1-4, 1Corinthians 1:30). The Law demands, but Grace supplies, because Jesus is the life-giver and His Gospel is life-giving (John 1:17, John 4:14).

Paul wrote to the Romans that their faith was being reported all over the world, but then immediately spoke of his longing to preach the gospel to them (Romans 1:15). Why did such faith-filled believers need the gospel? Because to Paul, the preaching of the gospel was nothing less than the impartation of the life of God's Spirit (Romans 1:8-17). We have gotten so used to preaching an earthly gospel (if you will give to God, then He will give to you) that we have settled for an earthly power: the power to motivate. Just because we place a beautiful worship session before a motivational talk, does not mean that the gospel has been preached!

The power Paul speaks of is not the eloquence of the speaker but the revelation of the presence of God through the speaker, their words carrying the authority of God and that unction opening eyes and hearts to the reality of the Kingdom and the King (1 Corinthians 2:4). Again, it is not just what is said but who is saying it. Authority trumps eloquence and emotion. It is not in volume or zeal we find the sign of God-given authority, but in the encounter with God's presence through the life of the one speaking.

Those who heard Jesus were struck by the authority with which He spoke, which was unlike anyone they had ever heard before (Matthew 7:29, John 7:46). He seemed to have an intimacy with God, a knowing of God that no man had ever had. He wasn't merely giving his opinion as an individual. It took a soldier to recognise this and articulate the source of Jesus' authority (Matthew 8:9, 10). He spoke with authority because he was living under authority, living a life submitted to God. Jesus Himself confirmed this when asked directly for the source of His authority. *"For I did not speak on my own, but the Father who sent me commanded me to say all that I have spoken."* (John 12:49).[125]

What is on display when people experience the authority of God through a speaker, is the intimacy of the speaker with the one of whom they speak. What is on display is nothing less than eternal life, for according to Jesus, it is such an intimate knowing of God that indeed is eternal life (John 17:3). We have been given the Holy Spirit so that we can live in such communion—live knowing and being known by God. We can live in the life-giving stream of His words to us, and this stream can also flow from us (Matthew 4:4, John 7:38). This is the scale of the generosity of our Father God. He offers us to share in His life today, not one day in the by and by.

---

[125] New International Version.

The gift the Gospel proclaims is not heaven one day, but the God who made heaven today! Heaven couldn't wait! The Gospel is both the invitation and the power to enter the feast, the communion of the Father and the Son through the Spirit. From the life that has entered in and taken their place at His table, emanates the sound of music and dancing, a liberty from the fear of death (Luke 15:25). We too, can only speak extraordinary words, to the extent that we are hearing such words. The life that bears such fruit, is the life that abides in such communion. (John 15:5).

It was this liberty (what can be described as a holy boldness) that marked the lives of the early church (Acts 4:13, Galatians 2:4). Such confidence was and is viewed as a threat by every earthly authority (religious and secular), because both use fear to control behaviour. No quantity of motivational talks or religious instruction can cast out fear. Only perfect love casts out fear, and a love of such quality is only found in the one who lays down His life for us, not on our best day but on our worst (1 John 4:18, Luke 23:34). Here is a love far beyond the transactional. Here is a love that embraces our sin and death and clothes us in His life and makes a place for us at His table. Here is a love that scandalizes any mind that is counting our sins against us (2 Corinthians 5:19). Here is a love that melts our hard hearts by dealing with the lie that hardened our hearts: the lie that our Father withheld His life from us and left us to save ourselves (Genesis 3:1-4). Here is a gospel for the powerless, in a world of performance.

The truth that sets us free is not merely His promise to us; it is His presence with us (John 14:6). Only the awareness of His life with us, transforms us into carriers of His presence, His light, into a world living in the darkness of separation. To speak with authority, is to speak as one living from union in a world of separation. It is to speak with the inexpressible and glorious joy of those who have never gotten over our amazement at how completely and freely He has shared His life with us. The exhortation to be continually being filled with His Spirit (Ephesians 5:18), is simply the recognition that this news is so good that no earthly religious mind can grasp it apart from the illumination of God's Spirit (1 Corinthians 2:14). Without the Holy Spirit taking hold of us and continually leading us into the depths of His love, our fears will inevitably carry our feet back towards the fields of religion, the safety of the separated life, where I save my 'self' through the strength of my life (Romans 10:1-5).

To be filled with His Spirit, is to begin to see yourself the way the Father sees you: hidden with Christ in God (Colossians 3:3). Such vision causes the Church to be filled with a joy inexpressible and full of glory, until she becomes so intoxicated by the generosity of His life, the life poured out, that from within her the light of His being rises again in a world shadowed by death. Once again, in the midst of our religious traditions and rituals, there can be an outpouring of a thanksgiving in the Church that causes us to live holier accidentally, than the most sin-conscious, self-absorbed zealot (Rom 10:1-4). Such is the life of those living from union in a world of separation.

This power to intoxicate is found in the gospel of God's love for us, not our love for Him, for *"this is love: not that we loved God, but that he loved us and sent his Son as an atoning sacrifice for our sins."*[126] (1 John 4:10). Religion (self-effort) only has the power to suffocate, for it will wrap you up so tight in yourself as to leave you as bound up as one wrapped for death (John 11:44). It will leave you waiting for eternal life one day.

The gospel is not the news that you might be saved one day, if you reconcile yourself to God by behaving better. That's not news. That's advice! The Gospel is the news that God in Christ reconciled you to Himself two thousand years ago and is now no longer counting your sins against you (2 Corinthians 5:19). Everyone else might still be counting your sins against you (including you), but the one person who isn't is your Father in heaven! He took the record of your attempts to save yourself (your sins) and nailed it

---

[126] New International Version.

to the Cross (Colossians 2:14, 15), for He never wanted His love for you to be shackled to your performance, no more than you would want your love for a child of yours to be limited by their performance.

Until you accept that, you will always be trying to do something about your sin. You will always be trying to deserve your way into your father's presence (Romans 10:1-4). If you don't put your pride in your back pocket and admit that even if you were given a thousand lifetimes, you could never make yourself as righteous as God is, and humble yourself and just accept the gift of His righteousness and the abundance of His grace (Romans 5:17), then you are always going to find yourself estranged from the joy of your Father. You will end up as miserable and self-righteous as that elder brother in Jesus' story of the prodigal son, because you are so determined to be your own Savour (Luke 15:28-30). Here's the gospel. For all who want a Saviour, you have one. If you want to be your own, then there is religion or atheism, but be warned again, it's the most miserable life in the world being your own Saviour! Might this in the end be why so many do not associate that sign "Gospel Service" with 'great joy'? They have met too many miserable Christians!

The Church must be amazed again at the gospel before the world can be (Acts 2:42, 43). Like Peter entering the house of Cornelius, we must speak as people amazed at the things we are saying, because we have been amazed at the things we are hearing. When we speak as those who are knowing intimacy with God, then our lives display the reality of eternal life (knowing God), and through such lives the Kingdom of Heaven is seen on the earth as a present reality, not a future possibility.

It is no accident that at the very beginning of His public ministry, Jesus went to his home synagogue in Capernaum and chose to read a passage from the prophet Isaiah that everyone present had always read as speaking of a future promise. *"The Spirit of the Lord is upon me, because He has anointed me to preach the gospel to the poor; He has sent me to heal the broken-hearted, to proclaim liberty to the captives and recovery of sight to the blind, to set at liberty those who are oppressed, and to proclaim the acceptable year of the Lord."* Then *He closed the book and gave it back to the attendant and sat down. And the eyes of all who were in the synagogue were fixed on Him. And He began to say to them, "Today this Scripture is fulfilled in your hearing."* [127](Luke 4:18-21)

The very first word Jesus declared to them was "Today!" The implications of that statement caused a riot, but the Holy Spirit is still given that the Kingdom of God can still be declared a present reality, for darkness does not flee from the promise of the dawn, but the presence.

---

[127] New King James Version.

Chapter Eleven
The Life of Obedience; His.

••••

Imagine a young pastor in Africa who marries his sweetheart. He and his wife remain very happy, but as the years go by, it becomes apparent that they cannot have children. They take medical advice, they pray and get all their friends to pray, but months turn into years, and they remain without children. Their constant prayer is, "Lord, we don't want to remain barren. We just want to bear fruit." The pastor's wife becomes very depressed.

One spring he leaves home to travel to another state. He is scheduled to lead an evangelistic campaign that will keep him away from home for 8 weeks. There is no phone coverage where he is going. When he finally returns home, his wife runs to greet him with the happy news that she is expecting. He has never seen her so happy. She proudly shares with him how she has been to the doctors that very week, and a scan has shown that she is six weeks pregnant. Shocked, the pastor replies, "But how can you be six weeks pregnant if I have been away for eight weeks?" She replies, "But what does that matter, compared to the fact that I have a child? After all, the goal was that I bear a child, right?" "Wrong!" her husband replies. "The goal was that we bear our child!"

Any religion that puts obedience before love, will be content with an obedience fathered by guilt, shame, or fear. Such fathers will never produce the obedience that the love of God conceives in us, the love of a parent for their children. To be filled with the Holy Spirit is to be filled with the love of the Father, a love that sees the stranger, even your enemy, as you would your own children (Luke 13:34). Such love always says the right thing and does the right thing. The actions of such love surpass mere obedience to commands, for such an obedience can be totally self-serving, whereas love is not self-seeking (1 Corinthians 13:5). Outward obedience to commands without an inner change of heart was what Jesus saw in the Pharisees. He called it a cleaning of the outside of the vessel while the inside remained full of greed and self-indulgence. (Matthew 23:25, 26).

As Christians too, we can be blind to the level of self-centredness that fuels our religious behaviour. I already described how disappointed I would be if it turned out that Nicola only married me to attain a better address, only resolved to become obedient to marriage, in order to attain her preferred home. Yet is that not the sort of obedience we risk producing when we reduce the gospel to a message about 'getting to heaven'? The Gospel is the revelation that heaven couldn't wait, for He who made heaven and earth came, that it would be on earth as it is in heaven (Matthew 6:10). The Gospel is the revelation that God's preferred home is not heaven, but the hearts of men (John 17:21). How does He feel about people inviting Jesus into their lives, so that they can 'get to heaven' one day? I am not diminishing the importance of such decisions, for Jesus promised that " *...whoever comes to me I will never drive away.*"[128] (John 6:37) But which is more valuable, Jesus or heaven? My point is that the Christian life is not one of merely waiting for heaven, but daily living in the presence of God (Colossians 3:3). We have not been left to come up with 'obedience' on our own because we have not

---

[128] New International Version.

been left on our own! We have been gifted the Spirit of Him whose obedience is selfless.

The obedience of God is an obedience unto death for the ones He loves. Jesus' obedience was not about Himself. His obedience served His Father's heart, which He shared. His obedience was never the master but always the servant of love. Jesus did not go to the Cross so that He would be made right, but so that we would be made right. The heart of God is an obedience fathered by love, not guilt or fear, and the Gospel is the only news that fills men with such a love that casts out fear. This is because only the Gospel can reveal us to be right in God's sight, not because we did the right thing, but because He did!

Do you know that the less Christians are filled with the love of God (the Spirit of God), the more they tend to emphasise obedience over love? Any ministry that emphasises obedience over love will see little wrong in using guilt and shame to try and motivate Christians into obedience. To them, it doesn't matter what you use to produce obedience, as long as the result is what appears to be obedience to God. But guilt, fear, and shame are the deadbeat dads of the spiritual world. They don't supply; they just keep on taking. They keep taking our eyes off how much we have been given in Christ, and so keep taking our joy and our thanksgiving.

But what if the result the Father wants for our lives is greater than obedience to God? What if he wanted more for us than for our lives to reveal our obedience? What if He wanted our lives to reveal His love? Obedience is a fundamental aspect of the life of Christ. His obedience took Him to death and through death, but His love for us was not birthed out of His obedience. It was the other way around. The root, the source of His obedience, was His love, which is His very nature (1 John 4:8). Obedience to God is the claim of many religious zealots who will even sacrifice their own lives. But in Christ we did not see a mere obedience to God; we saw the obedience of God, an obedience that does not take life but gives life. Any sacrificial life of obedience to God that is not birthed by the love of God is ultimately self-serving. It will leave us like the prodigal son's elder brother, estranged and angry that all our sacrifice has not brought us what we hoped it would (Luke 15:28, 29; 1 Corinthians 13:3).

God's plan was not to send Christ to live an exemplary life, a life that He now expects us to try and imitate through obedience. Christ was not sent to motivate us but to save us! God never had a plan to save the world through our obedience. His plan was to save the world through His love. His plan was to impart His love (His nature) into us, by pouring into our hearts His very Spirit, His very life, so that men and women filled with the love of God, the Spirit of God, the life of God, can go out into the world and renew the world, by bringing the revelation of the infinite worth of each person: Christ crucified.

His plan for us was never to merely change our behaviour, but to change our fundamental beliefs. He wasn't after the branches, but the root of our lives, our hearts. Adam thought he only needed a new tailor (Genesis 3:7). God saw he needed a heart transplant surgeon! (Ezekiel 36:26, 27)

To God, obedience was never something that we bring to Him as if we have made it ourselves (Genesis 4:3-5). The only obedience that pleases God is that which His love has birthed in our lives. This is an obedience that is of the Spirit, that is the gift of God. Obedience is not about willpower but about a will empowered by the Spirit of God. Jesus told Nicodemus that flesh always gives birth to flesh (John 3:6). Obedience that is birthed out of a life filled with the fear of rejection, will never lead to the character of Christ. Jesus was not moved by a self-centred fear. He didn't come to save His life, but to lay it down for us (John 10:18). He told His disciples this when they tried to prevent His arrest in the garden of Gethsemane (Matthew 26:53).

The obedience of the religious in Jesus' day led only to pride and division. It was that sort of obedience to God that persecuted and then crucified Christ. Any religion that is blind to what Christ accomplished on the Cross, will always ask for your obedience in a way that implies that your obedience will bring you closer to God. Here is the Gospel. Believer, in Christ you cannot get closer to God! Through Christ you died, and your life is now hidden with Christ in God (Colossians 3:3).

To believe in Christ is to be born from above (John 3:3). For every believer, heaven is not your finishing line; it is your starting place! The more that Christians start to live from there (abide in their union with Christ in God), the more the Kingdom of Heaven will be seen on the earth (John 15:4, 5). The more His heart becomes our heart, the more we come to understand that His desire was never to merely fill heaven with obedient servants, but to fill the earth with loving sons (Matthew 6:10, Romans 8:29).

This union with Christ in God means that for a Christian there is no longer 'your' obedience, in the sense that you have been left alone to produce obedience by yourself. You do not have that sort of life anymore, an 'alone by yourself' life, a life that boasts that "I" have been obedient. Instead, every Christian should be able to say what the apostle Paul said, *"I am crucified with Christ: nevertheless I live; yet not I, but Christ liveth in me: and the life which I now live in the flesh I live by the faith of the Son of God, who loved me, and gave himself for me."*[129] (Gal 2:20) The obedience of the believer arises from their union with God in Christ, not from their separation from Him.

The root meaning of the Greek word translated in the New Testament as obedience, *'hypakoē'* means *'to listen attentively.'*[130] Biblical obedience implies relationship; that we are close enough to someone to hear what they are saying (Matthew 8:8, 9). Jesus didn't say, 'My sheep read about me.' He said, *"My sheep hear my voice."*[131] (John 10:27). True obedience always has its source in God.

---

[129] King James Bible.
[130] Strongs Number G5218. https://www.blueletterbible.org/lexicon/g5218/kjv/tr/0-1/
[131] New King James Version.

We no more have an 'independent' obedience than we have an independent righteousness, a self-made righteousness. Nothing 'of ourselves' makes us righteous (Ephesians 2:8, 9). That includes our obedience. God's plan was never to make men righteous through their obedience but through His, which is why the apostle Paul boldly declared to the Romans that *"through the obedience of the one man the many will be made righteous."*[132] (Romans. 5:19). Here is the news that sets you free from religious self-effort: that one man is not you. It is Jesus Christ. Yes, we are made righteous by obedience—His!

God's way of saving us was not by giving us instructions to obey, but by giving us Himself. Grace and truth weren't some things God gave. The apostle John declared that grace and truth came in the person of Jesus (John 1:17), for in Him was life and the light of all mankind (John 1:4). Christ did not come to stand back from us. He did not come to stand on the shore issuing instructions to a drowning mankind on how to swim better towards Him. He came to unite His life with ours and go down with us into death, so that we might rise with Him into eternal life (Romans 6:5).

Your life and mine is an open book to the world as to whose obedience we are relying on and operating in. Let your faith be rooted in His obedience, His life, and what will grow in your life is the righteousness of God. If you let religion, the spirit of the world, the spirit that says, "You can do it," subtly move your faith off His obedience onto yours, then more and more what this world will see in your life is not God's righteousness but self-righteousness and all the division and finger-pointing that goes with it (Galatians 5:13-15). If the gospel we have been sitting under for years has, in all honesty, produced a church of self-righteous believers who love to label people and type them according to their level of obedience to God's commands, then somewhere along the road we have been

---

[132] New International Version.

robbed of the power of the gospel. We may have been raised under such a gospel, but we have not been raised by it!

The power of the gospel is that it reveals the righteousness of God to be the gift of God (Romans 1:16, 17), and that very revelation—that Christ has become for us our righteousness, our holiness, our redemption (1 Corinthians 1:30)—sets us free from the power of sin and death, for that came through the lie that we could be like God by ourselves. God never had a plan to save the world through our obedience. His plan was to save the world through His love.

Let me use another illustration that may help communicate better what I mean when I say that God always purposed for our lives to be rooted in the obedience of God, rather than our obedience to God. I am not saying that obedience to God is unimportant. My obedience to the call to get up each morning and work hard and make sacrifices to serve my family with the best life I can give to them is not unimportant; it is very important. But that obedience is not birthed from a desire to get closer to my family or to get something from them. That obedience is birthed and grows purely out of my love for my family. The obedience of God in our lives is the work of His Spirit, His nature, His love in our hearts, from which obedience is birthed. Obedience is only pleasing to God if His love is the root, the source of that obedience. Let me put that another way. Obedience is only pleasing to God, if He is the Father of that obedience.

Imagine one day you find yourself in a crowd of people when suddenly the attention of this crowd is drawn to a gang of men. This gang has set upon a young man in broad daylight and is beating him with baseball bats. These men are so angry and violent that the crowd draws back in fear. Now what do you do as a Christian?

Let's be honest, the first thing we do is hesitate. In that moment of hesitation, in our minds we can hear the command of God to love others, to be willing to lay down our lives for them. In those moments we begin to attempt to engage our will, to try and muster up the courage to be obedient to God's commands. After all, that is all a Christian is, right? Someone who obeys God? Wrong! Let me show you whom God truly calls us to be, and by His Spirit equips us to be.

Imagine in those first few seconds, while you or I hesitate and try and muster up the courage to do something about the man being beaten, suddenly we see an older woman from the crowd running towards the gang. We watch her throw herself over the young man to shield him from the blows, even taking the blows herself. While you and I hesitated because we were relying on obedience, this woman did not hesitate because she had something much more powerful coursing through every fibre of her being. She was filled with the love of a mother for her son!

Jesus spoke so much about the heart of the Father. But as He drew nearer Jerusalem and approached the time to lay His body over ours and take the blows of sin and death that were meant for us, suddenly He began to describe the love He felt in His heart, as like that of a mother towards her children. He looked down on Jerusalem and lamented over her, saying, *"How often I wanted to gather your children together, the way a hen gathers her chicks under her wings and you were unwilling."*[133] (Matthew 23:37).

God's way of bringing forth His life in us, is not to rely on our obedience to commands, but to fill us with His love, a love that sees the stranger as you would your own child. It is only the Holy Spirit that pours this love into our hearts, and this love, the love of the Father, conceives and brings forth the obedience of God in our lives.

Some say that true love demands a response, but God did not merely demand a response from Mary. His love conceived and bore a response in her, because she received that love. She let herself be so loved, for her heart cried, *"Be it unto me according to thy word"*[134] (Luke 1:38). In His word to her was the power to 'let it be'.

---

[133] New American Standard Bible.
[134] King James Bible.

It is His Word going forth that renews the earth and our hearts (Acts 16:14, 1 Corinthians 12:3). God never expected that we could believe apart from Him, or be obedient apart from Him, for 'apart from Him' is death. How many dead men have you heard commended on their obedience? Obedience is only pleasing to God if He; Love, is the father of that obedience. Love is a better father of obedience than fear, or guilt, or shame because love never fails to do the right thing (1 Corinthians 13:8).

We all want to be found obedient to the call of God and the Spirit of God in our lives.

We all want to do the right thing, but God never saw you or I as having to rely on willpower alone to be obedient. He always saw obedience as the fruit His love conceives in us, for love always does the right thing.

Let's think about another illustration of selfless obedience. A young woman who is about to become a mother for the first time, may have genuine fears about whether she is able to face such a challenge. Will she be able to always do the right thing for her child? She may think that others would make a much better mother than her. But from the moment that baby is put in her arms, she is filled with so much love for her child that she handles and cares for that child with a tenderness, a dedication, and a selflessness that no one else in the world can match. That's because no one loves you like your mother! That love she has for her child informs and directs everything she does, even to the laying down of her life for her child.

My wife, Nicola, is one of the quietest and gentlest people I have ever known. But there have been incidents down the years when something or someone looks like they are going to harm one of our children. In those moments I have seen her rise like a lion and step between her child and the threat. She steps up and says, in effect, "You are going to have to go through me to get to them." No wonder Jesus, on His way to the Cross, described himself as like a mother hen who just wanted to gather her chicks under her wings (Matthew

23:37). Christ on the Cross is God declaring to sin and death, "You are going to have to go through me to get to them!"

Here is the good news: they could not get through Him! When darkness met light, light won. When union met separation, union won. When sin and death met Christ on that Cross, the communion of Father, Son, and Holy Spirit, the union of the Trinity was stronger than the separation of sin and death (Psalm 22:24, Colossians 1:17).

The resurrection of Christ was the appearing of this victory and the proclamation that the way was now open—the way for men and women to live in and live from the communion of the Father and Son in the Spirit. That way was Christ. All who receive Him find they have received the power and authority to live as children of God, to live no longer intimidated by death but to live from eternal life (John 1:12). They can live fully in each day, no longer grasping for life in the shadow of death, but living by the light of the life they find their spirits in union with (Ephesians 5:8).

They find this light to be brighter than the sun, in that even death, the tyrant of this natural world, pales before it. In being filled with this light, the eternal life of God, they find themselves no longer shackled to an earthly timeline, for in Christ they died with Him and rose with Him and are now seated with Him. In the light of His glory and grace, they also find, (just as the old hymn promised), the things of this earth growing strangely dim, and to their amazement, one of those things is death! They find that what had always kept them shackled to an earthly life, their fear of death, Christ has now freed them from (Hebrews 2:15).

As young David ran towards Goliath, it looked to earthly eyes that he was running towards death. Yet those close enough would have been astonished to hear that as he ran, he was rebuking the giant before him and speaking to him as if he was already dead! (1 Samuel 17:45-47). So too the life and the confession of the Christian is empowered by the Holy Spirit to be a prophecy of the death of death. The pouring into our hearts of the love of God casts out the fear of death, and our lives begin to outshine any glory of a passing-away world cowering in the shadow of death. As we run our race towards that giant, let those close to us hear us also rebuke the giant and prophesy his demise. Let the way we live our lives call out, *"O death, where is thy sting? O grave, where is thy victory? ... But thanks be to God, which giveth us the victory through our Lord Jesus Christ."*[135] (1 Corinthians 15:55, 57).

Your obedience is not the foundation of your righteousness, your life in God. Christ's obedience is. Despite the fact that you may have heard a thousand messages in church emphasising your obedience to God over and over again, no preacher has the right to lay any foundation to your new life in Christ, other than the one already laid. Those aren't my words, but those of the apostle Paul to the Corinthians, recorded in 1 Corinthians 3:10, 11. *"By the grace God has given me, I laid a foundation as a wise builder, and someone else is building on it. But each one should build with care. For no one can lay any foundation other than the one already laid, which is Jesus Christ."*[136]

The reason why so many of us approach the Bible like a self-help instruction manual, is because too much of our weight is leaning on the wrong place. Rather than the weight of our salvation resting entirely in Christ and His finished work, someone has mixed us and our obedience, into the foundation. What happens when you mix a foreign mineral into the concrete of a house's foundation? Over the last 20 years in the northwest of Ireland, thousands of people have watched as their homes have literally begun to crack and disintegrate over time. These homes were built with too much of a mineral called Mica mixed into the concrete. For the first few years all appeared normal, for it takes a few years for the Mica to begin to draw in water from the outside environment. This begins to swell the concrete in places and so weaken its cohesiveness. Within a few years, the first signs that appear are cracks in the walls and floors.

What happens when someone keeps adding your performance

---

[135] King James Bible.
[136] New International Version.

as an individual into the finished work of Christ as the foundation for your salvation? Nothing to begin with. But before long, because you are putting far too much weight on something as weak as your willpower, cracks will start to appear. You will either swell up with pride that your obedience has been good enough to gain you salvation. Or you will slide into despair, as you see your own willpower let you down again and again.

When a congregation knows that their salvation sits on the foundation of Christ and His obedience, that as Ephesians 2:8, 9 declares, we are saved by grace through faith and this not of themselves but is the gift of God, lest any man should boast" there is established a great unity and cohesiveness in that body of people. This is because no one is sitting in judgment on anyone else or looking to their own performance or anyone else's for their hope of salvation. Everyone's eyes are fixed on Christ, who is the author and the finisher of our faith (Hebrews 12:2).

This is why it is so important to preach the Gospel of Christ's finished work every Sunday. We keep the mica of 'self' out of the foundation of our new lives, so that we don't start cracking up and dividing because our hope has slipped from Christ onto people. I thank God that my hope is not in any church or any minister, or I might end up disappointed or disillusioned. I am trusting that if we keep sitting under the preaching of the Gospel that lifts up Christ and His work, then when people let us down (and they will), our lives do not begin to crack and totter because the foundation laid in them was Christ and His work, not anyone else's. It is only in Him that all things hold together (Colossians 1:17).

If a congregation's hope is on me and my performance as a pastor, then I have been laying the wrong foundation. Sooner or later cracks are going to appear because there is only one man good enough to carry the weight of your life, and that is Christ. I am emphasising this as it is a sad experience to know believers who have ended their days divided and disappointed because the weight of their expectations had slipped off Christ and onto personalities or some earthly organisation. All because someone laid a foundation in their lives other than Christ (1 Corinthians 3:1-11).

We were not born again by the strength of our will, but by the will of God (John 1:13). Your life as a believer was not birthed and cannot rest on the strength of your willpower alone, your obedience alone. But the danger is that if leaders keep relentlessly pointing you to your obedience, you may well start to think that your obedience is the foundation for your salvation. The truth is that your obedience cannot exist alone. It is the fruit of the foundation laid in your life: Christ, a foundation that was laid when God spoke to you, through the Gospel of Christ's finished work, not your unfinished work. It was He who began this great work in you, not you, and it is He who will complete it (Philippians 1:6, Galatians 3:3).

It was no accident that crucifixion was the manner of Christ's death, for it is the only death where a man dies with his arms outstretched. Yet in that same passage of scripture, where Jesus describes Himself as like a mother hen wanting to gather her chicks under her wings, He is weeping over Jerusalem. He is weeping because He says that they were unwilling to be gathered. (Matthew 23:37). The Lord does not force anyone to receive this new life against their will because love doesn't force. Love *"does not seek its own benefit."*[137] (1 Corinthians 13:5). Love stretched out His arms for the whole world and invites all into His love. His love is like light. When you allow His light into your life and live in this light, you find that it is His light, His love, that deals with all the shadows of darkness in your life: the fears, the loneliness, the anger, and the lusts of a life lived cut off from the love of God.

The Lord is not asking you to clean your life up to a certain standard before He will commit Himself to you, for He never expected that you could clean your life of darkness. That is the job of the light, the love of God, the presence of His Spirit in your life. As Christ, the sun of righteousness rises in our lives (Malachi

---

[137] New American Standard Bible.

4:2), His rising life deals with the unbelief, the false picture of the Father, the darkness at the root of our lives, by persuading our hearts that we are indeed God's children (Romans 8:16). It is His life rising in us that causes our lives to shine like stars in a generation darkened by unbelief (Philippians 2:15). In Christ, we live from union in a world of separation. We were never called to conceive an obedience of our own, for the life of obedience the world needs to see, is His!

Chapter Twelve

Heavenly Government: the empowerment to be.

· · · ·

Several years ago, at the start of the Covid pandemic, my thoughts kept returning to how our grandparents faced a worldwide crisis that was much worse. During the Second World War, eighty million people died in a struggle that went on for six years. During those years people suffered incredible hardships, especially if you lived in a country where cities were being bombed. I remember as a child being fascinated by a documentary series called 'The World at War.' It was made in Britain, so part of it documented the rationing and the restrictions that were imposed on the people there and the effect on their lives of living in fear for so long. It recorded how the government, desperate to achieve victory, sought to mobilise the whole nation to sacrificial living. This meant that for six years, nearly every government announcement in Britain was an instruction of some sort, as to what people needed to do and keep doing, if victory was to be achieved. During those war years, the public only heard announcements on what they needed to do, in order to become victorious.

But everything changed on May 8th, 1945. On that date a

different announcement was made, one that was so different that it transformed the nation. They even gave that date a special name, VE Day (Victory in Europe Day). It was the announcement that the war was over, that victory was no longer a future hope but finally a present reality. At this announcement a great celebration began. For several days the whole nation danced and sang and gave thanks, as 'doing to become' had finally been replaced by being!

Of all the thousands of government announcements during those six long years, none had had that effect before. None had caused such an outbreak of joy. That's because for six years every government message to the people was one of instruction—a message about what they needed to do, to become victorious. All those announcements effectively said the same thing: "In order for you to become, this is what you need to do." But the message that started the nationwide party was different. It did not say, "In order for you to become, this is what you need to do." It said, "This is who you are, because of what has been done!" Today you are victorious. Today you are free because of what has been done.

Now listen to how the apostle Paul described the ministry of the Holy Spirit to the Romans. *"The Spirit himself testifies with our spirit that we are God's children."*[138] (Romans.8:16). Can you see it yet? Good news is always the news of what is, not what might be! All the other government announcements throughout the war spoke of a life in the future, a life that people should live for. But that announcement on VE Day spoke of a different life; not a life in the future that people should live for, but a life today that people could live from and could live in. Millions immediately began to live in that new life, in the joy of it and in the peace of it, because they believed the announcement.

That angel at the incarnation did not bring the shepherds a heavenly government advice announcement. The gospel is the announcement of good news, not good advice, because it is not a

---

[138] New International Version.

message of what will be if you first. It is the declaration of what is, because Christ first! It is not more instruction for a world already being advised to death. It is news, news that a victory has now been achieved that can be lived from, not just lived for.

That victory in 1945 marked the end in the UK of a government of war and the beginning of a government of peace. The New Testament speaks of what governs our mind as determining how we live: *"The mind governed by the flesh is death, but the mind governed by the Spirit is life and peace."*[139] (Romans 8:6) If we do not allow the news that Christ has defeated sin and death to reign in our lives, then we cannot live from the peace of God. If the God you are believing in is not at peace, then neither will you ever be!

In Christ, we have the life that lives from God, not just for God. It is God's will that through His Church, His Kingdom of peace will be seen on earth as it is in heaven (Matthew 6:10). In light of the resurrection of Christ, we can live set free from the fear of death (Hebrews 2:15). The resurrection is the news that death pales before, for it is the announcement of the defeat of sin and death (1 Corinthians 15:55-57, 2 Timothy 1:10) and the appearance of a new immortal life, the life hidden with Christ in God (Colossians 3:1-4).

It is the presence of His Holy Spirit in our lives that illuminates our hearts to believe the naturally unbelievable: that we can now live under a new rule, a new government of peace, no longer living in fear of death and so no longer grasping for life (Hebrews 2:15). In the words of the apostle Peter, we can now partake in the divine nature and shine in this world because we have *"escaped the corruption in this world caused by evil desires"*[140] (2 Peter 1:4). Without knowing their Saviour, every person attempts to save themselves, and a world seeking to save itself, is a world full of evil desires.

This is why a world so darkened by the fear of death, needs the light of the Gospel. On those living in the shadow of death, a light

---

[139] New International Version.
[140] New International Version.

has dawned, and that light, the revelation of God in the face of Christ, calls us and empowers us to live in the light of knowing God. To know Him as the life-giver, is to live in His given life, Christ. It is to live in the light of eternal life (John 17:3). This is news on such a seismic scale that, just like that announcement on VE Day, it has the power to release people into a new life; no longer a 'doing to become' life, but a life of 'being,' being in victory, being in peace, being in God!

No wonder Paul said he was determined to preach nothing but Christ and Him crucified (1 Corinthians 2:2), for he knew that to point people to themselves as their hope, was no hope at all, no gospel at all (Galatians 1:6, 7). Pointing me to myself is not good news. Paul discovered that when people hear the gospel as the news of what has been done for them, rather than advice on what they should do for God, they are empowered by that news to live from and live in what has been done for them, Christ's given life. In other words, the message itself empowers people to live a new life. Listen once more to how he said this to the Romans. *"For I am not ashamed of the gospel, for it is the power of God for salvation to everyone who believes."*[141] (Romans 1:16).

The Gospel is the power of God to save because the power of God is His Spirit, and His Spirit rests on (anoints) the truth of what is, not what might be! The Spirit witnesses with the truth of what is, because of what Christ did. He always points us to Christ and His finished work, not to us and our unfinished works, for He knows our faith can rest on Christ, but not on ourselves. True Gospel preaching leaves our faith resting on Christ and His sinless life, not on us and our sinning-less life! Religion (self-effort) will give us no rest and tired people can be miserable! No matter how many scriptures have been used to justify a message, always ask yourself this question: did what I just hear leave my hope on Christ or on me?

Because God's Spirit speaks of what is, He speaks to us as a

---

[141] New American Standard Bible.

father would, one who sees who we are and speaks to us as who we are. The Spirit doesn't see us and so doesn't speak to us as a manager or an employer would. They are both productivity-focused and so can't help always speaking to us about what we should do, in order to become someone better, someone more productive for God. Notice the heavenly Gospel speaks of life in God, whereas earthly religion tends to speak of life for God.

Even though he believed that the recipients of his letter already knew the truths he was teaching, the apostle Peter insisted on reminding them (2 Peter 1:12). Repetition is a fundamental aspect of raising lives to maturity. In a world that is constantly promising us who we could be one day, it is important we recognise that announcements that originate from the heavenly government empower us to find our being in Christ, not our becoming (Acts 17:28). The Spirit testifies to what is, not what might be. He always speaks to us as who we are, not who we could be. *"The Spirit himself testifies with our spirit that we are God's children."*[142] (Romans 8:16).

Many of us have thought of prophecy primarily in terms of the Spirit speaking of things that are to come, foretelling. But in reality, (heaven's reality), the Holy Spirit is speaking of things that are true. He is thus more forthtelling, telling forth what is, in order that it be believed. Through this heavenly gospel, the gift of faith comes, for no man can say Jesus is Lord apart from God's Spirit (1 Corinthians 12:3). As men's and women's eyes are opened to see the reality that God sees, so their mouths are opened to speak God's reality, and so His Kingdom comes on earth as it is in heaven (Acts 2:4-12, Acts 10:44-46).

Heaven saw Saul of Tarsus on his way to Damascus to persecute Christians, as God's chosen vessel to bring the gospel to the Gentiles (Acts 9:15). But no-one on the earth saw that heavenly reality. When the Holy Spirit told a disciple in Damascus called Ananias to go and pray for Saul, Ananias was so appalled he began speaking

---

[142] New International Version.

to God as if he knew things about Saul that God didn't. "Lord," Ananias answered, "*I have heard many reports about this man and all the harm he has done to your holy people in Jerusalem. And he has come here with authority from the chief priests to arrest all who call on your name.*"[143] (Acts 9:13, 14). I must admit to often praying in the same way, as if God doesn't quite understand how difficult things are 'down here'!

To Ananias, Saul is the one who is harming the Church. (Acts 9:13, 14). But in His response to Ananias, listen to whom the Lord declares Saul to be. "*This man is my chosen instrument to proclaim my name to the Gentiles and their kings and to the people of Israel.*"[144] (Acts 9:15) Ananias could never have perceived this reality, heaven's reality, apart from this revelation of the Holy Spirit. He had said to God in effect, "But this man *is* …" God's response was to declare, "No, this man *is* …" The power of God's 'is' prevails over Ananias' 'is'.

Ananias finds himself empowered by this revelation to carry God's reality, the heavenly 'is' into the earth, and that is what he did. In the power of the Spirit, in the power of what is true in God, he walked up to his arch enemy, placed his hand on him, and the first word out of his mouth was, "*Brother!*"[145] (Acts 9:17) In effect he was saying, "Brother Saul, here is who God declares you to be," and in that declaration of what is, that declaration of God's reality, came the power of the Holy Spirit (Acts 9:18).

That power caused something like scales to fall from Saul's eyes, and he could see again, only this time he saw things totally differently, for he saw himself as God saw him, and from that point he lived the life God always saw him living: the life of a son of God, for those who are led by the Spirit of God, (those who see the reality the Spirit sees), can live as the sons of God (Romans 8:14). From heaven's perspective, the Gospel and the Spirit are in complete

---

[143] New International Version.
[144] New International Version.
[145] New International Version.

agreement. They both speak of what is, that we may believe and live in what is: God's given life, communion with the Father and the Son in the Spirit (John 17:20-23).

If you were living in London during the war, then what you heard on VE Day was not an announcement of who you could be, but of who you are because of what has been done for you. You would have found that with the proclamation of such news, came the liberty to live in that new reality, the reality of who you now are because of what has been done for you. You didn't have to go back to working harder in the hope that you may be free one day.

So too in the proclamation of the Gospel comes the power to live in your new freedom, your new life, your 'hidden with Christ in God' life immediately, because the Spirit is present to enable you to live as a child of God. He does this by testifying to your Spirit, that you are a child of God (Romans 8:14-16). Now yes, there follows a journey to grow up into this life, what Ephesians calls 'growing up into Christ' (Ephesians 4:11-15), but believer, you cannot grow up in a life unless you have already been birthed into that life (John 3:5-8). In Christ, you are not becoming a new creation; you are declared to already be one. In Christ, old things are not passing away and new things are on the way. In Christ, *"old things have passed away; behold, all things have become new"*.[146] (2 Corinthians 5:17).

Being who God has made us to be, starts with seeing whom God has made us to be. Paul said that the message we declare is that God has reconciled the world to Himself and is now no longer counting their sins against them (2 Corinthians 5:19). He called this announcement the message of reconciliation and us the ministers of that reconciliation (2 Corinthians 5:18, 19). Again, reconciliation is not a work to be achieved, but a work to be believed! Every earthly religion will instruct you on how you can reconcile yourself to God. But notice the message of the Gospel is not 'do' reconciliation, but

---

[146] New King James Version.

'be' reconciled. *"We implore you on Christ's behalf, be reconciled to God."*[147] (2 Corinthians 5:20).

Mary's response to God's will was not "Let me do what needs to be done," but *"Let it be to me according to your word."*[148] (Luke 1:38). Our Father in heaven no more wants people to say, "Let me do," than the father in Jesus' parable of the prodigal son. When his son said, *"Please take me on as a hired servant."*[149] (Luke 15:19) the father realised his son was still 'doing to become' and needed to find his being as a son. This is why He immediately began to give his life to him as only a father gives to his son, not his servant (Luke 15:22, 23). When that son chose to accept what his father was giving and entered into his father's joy, he was choosing to *"Let it be to me according to your word"*[150] (Luke 1:38) There is nothing wrong with serving our heavenly father through hard work, as long as we serve as a son born of our father's love, not as a servant seeking to save himself. In Christ we are children of God through faith, but not faith in our work, but Christ's (Galatians 3:26-29).

The world began to live in peace after 1945, because they believed the announcement of what had been accomplished. They believed the announcement, "It is finished". However, there was at least one Japanese soldier who could not live in peace because he refused to believe the announcement. He fought on for years, launching attacks from a hiding place deep in the jungle of the Philippines. At first, he could not live in the peace provided because he had not heard the announcement. But in later years he still could not live in the peace provided because he refused to believe the announcement. We can do nothing about people refusing to believe the announcement, but we can do something about people who have never heard the announcement. Listen to what Paul said in Romans 10:14, 15. *"How will they believe in Him whom they have not heard? And how will they*

---

[147] New International Version.
[148] New King James Version.
[149] New Living Translation.
[150] New King James Version.

hear without a preacher? How will they preach unless they are sent? Just as it is written, "How beautiful are the feet of those who bring good news of good things!"[151] What a wonderful description of the Gospel: good news of good things. It is good news of good things because it is the announcement of the good things God has done, not the good things you need to do. That's why it is good news, not good advice.

The Church can only rise and shine in the light of what is (Proverbs 13:12). We were not called to build on what might be, but on what is. The Church needs to see again that the power of heaven is not found in the excellence of our plans, but in the foolishness of our message. (1 Corinthians 1:18, 2 Corinthians 12:10). How foolish, to sing in the dark as if you are standing in the noonday sun (Acts 16:25). But to hear the Gospel proclaimed in the power of the Spirit is not to hear a message about the future but about the present. It is to hear that your light has come and that the glory of the Lord has already risen on you. It is to hear that in the day when darkness covers the earth and deep darkness the peoples, we can arise and shine, for His glory has appeared in us. When the Church arises in the light of what is, she proclaims the gospel on earth as it is in heaven, and nations come to her light and kings to the brightness of her rising (Isaiah 60:1-3). This is the rising Church, a people awakened by the light of the gospel of what is, to arise into the life that now is, the life that dawned at the resurrection, hidden with Christ in God.

As the Church receives the *'euangelion,'* the good announcement of a great victory, she awakens to the news of a finished work. She finds indeed that *'hope deferred makes the heart sick, but a dream fulfilled is a tree of life'*[152] (Proverbs 13:12). She finds a joy rising, inexpressible and full of glory, and that her feet, once crippled by sin and death, now have the power to leap and dance their way into the presence of God (Acts 3:7, 8). She finds herself alive to a new

---

[151] New King James Version.
[152] New Living Translation.

government, a new kingdom, and it is a kingdom of righteousness, peace, and joy in the Holy Spirit (Romans 14:17). She finds herself in VE Day, Victory on Earth Day, for in Christ the Kingdom has come on earth as it is in heaven. Old things have passed away, and all things have become new (2 Corinthians 5:17).

Our warfare is the sound of our laughter and worship, for victory has dawned. We who were dead are alive. We who were prisoners have been made free. We who were blind can now see. We who had sat in darkness have seen a great light, and in receiving His light, we find ourselves living, moving, and finding our being in Him (Acts 17:28), our faces reflecting His (Acts 6:15, 2 Corinthians 3:18). This was always His intention, that the face of the Father would be seen in His children, that this world would come under a new government, His countenance of peace (Numbers 6:24-26).

Chapter Thirteen

The Dawn that death flees from.

· · · ·

The 22nd of August 2022 was a special day for our family. It was my father's 90th birthday, and he was determined to celebrate the occasion by inviting as many of his family and friends as he could to a meal at a local hotel. His original handwritten list had contained over 160 names! We were all still emerging from two years of social distancing, and this was going to be the first time there had been such a large reunion of family. Now your concept of family and mine may differ somewhat. My father is one of six brothers and five sisters, and I have never been able to remember all my cousins' names! It turned out to be a memorable night, with Dad fulfilling his wish to make a speech of thanksgiving for his life and inviting everyone to return for his 100th! It was also a special celebration for another reason: there was no loud music or dancing. After two years of being kept apart, everyone just wants to taste again the simple pleasure of being together around a table! Absence had indeed only made the heart grow fonder. There was such a joy in that room as we all rediscovered the power of presence, of being found together with the ones you love. We are made for such communion because all family life springs from our heavenly father, from whom every family in heaven and earth derives its name (Ephesians 3:14, 15).

At the heart of our lives are the issues of absence and presence. It was Abraham who cried out to God for his son Ishmael, for he recognised that his son was living unaware of the presence of God (Genesis 17:18), and the absence of such awareness was leaving him grasping for life (Genesis 16:12). Many Christians get nervous when you start to talk about grace because, in their minds, grace speaks of an absence, the absence of God's judgment. But grace is not an absence, grace is a presence—the presence of God (John 1:17). Grace is His life, His Spirit, His empowering to live His life. The Gospel is the good news that through Christ, His grace is now freely available for all who want to live in the power of His life. For all who want to live in the power of their own life, there is religion (self-effort) (Romans 10:1-4).

In his letter to the Galatians, the apostle Paul was clear that you cannot mix the two. Add a little religion to your gospel, and you will shrink it of power. That's why as soon as Paul heard that the Galatians had tampered with the gospel, he started to question them about where exactly they thought the power came from by which miracles had been done in their midst. He asked them, *"So then, does He who provides you with the Spirit and works miracles among you, do it by works of the Law, or by hearing with faith?"*[153] (Galatians 3:5) Can you hear what he was asking them? Does power come from hearing what you need to give God, or hearing what God has given you? He was warning them that in adding a little self-effort to the message, they had just diminished the power of the gospel, because there is no power in any gospel that points you to yourself. Being told what to do never set anyone free, because being pointed to yourself can never set you free from yourself.

The Gospel is not a revelation of what you need to do, to get God to give! The Gospel is the glorious revelation of the enormity of how

---

[153] New American Standard Bible.

much God has already given, and to see how much, to see "His only son," is to see the Father in spirit and in truth. The Gospel doesn't point to you and say, "Do!" It points to Christ and says, "Done!" It doesn't point us to the darkness of self-effort. It points us to the light of Christ, and when we see by His light (when we see life in the light of how much we have been given), we see ourselves to already have all things in Christ (1 Corinthians 3:21). Such knowledge takes an axe to the root of our grasping, selfish life, for only when we see that our Father has already saved us through the gift of His son, can we stop trying to save ourselves. The apostle Peter described the power of partaking of God's life as "*having escaped the corruption that is in the world on account of lust*".[154] (2 Peter 1:4). When you have been created to partake of God, that is a thirst for life that nothing in this world is going to satiate! That is a thirst of infinite proportions (Ecclesiastes 3:11). Religion (self-effort) is never going to satisfy that thirst, and when we deprive people of the gospel of God's grace, we only leave them thirsty enough to go back into the world looking for a drink.

The power of the Gospel is that it reveals the righteousness of God; His eternal life, is not some 'thing' we achieve, but some 'one' we receive. Christ is the gift of God's life, not the reward for our life. There can be no mixing of receiving and achieving when it comes to the Gospel. No matter how zealous they were for God, in praying and fasting and sacrificial living, Paul said in Romans 10 that his Jewish brethren could not submit to receive the gift of God's righteousness, Christ, because they were so determined to establish their own righteousness (Romans 10:1-4).

To sin is to live looking to yourself for life. It is to live the single life, the alone life. It is a life turned in on itself and away from God. Any message that throws you back onto your own effort is tempting you to sin. Any message that points you to Christ and the sufficiency of His work for all your needs, is making you more alive to God

---

[154] New American Standard Bible.

and dead to sin. Can you see then, that grace is not a licence to sin; religion is! Grace is the power of God to live in union with Him. We can only live in that power of His grace to the extent that we submit to receive and live in God's life entirely as a gift. We must let His gospel put our striving hearts to rest. God put the first Adam to sleep so that He could bring from his side a new life: Eve. On the Cross the last Adam went to sleep, at rest in His Father's ability to save Him, and from Him, too, came new life, a new creation: the Church, the bride of Christ sharing the life of Christ (John 12:24).

It is from rest that new life flows. Our Father is described as at rest and calling His children into His rest (Hebrews 4:10). In Jesus' parable of the prodigal son, the father insists that the son's restored life begin in a feast, a resting and rejoicing. This is what enrages the elder son. He sees such rest as a reward for all his works, not the source of it, for his hope has always been in himself. He can't join in the celebration, as being his own saviour has made him too miserable! He needs to know that all that he is trying to work for in his own strength is already his by the gift of his father. It is the need to tell him this that brings the father himself out into the fields.

Today, through the person of the Holy Spirit, our Father is still coming out into the fields of religion, to plead with men to come to the end of their works and enter into the rest He has provided, the life of His Son. Listen to the way this is stated in Hebrews 4:9-11. *"There remains, then, a Sabbath-rest for the people of God; for anyone who enters God's rest also rests from their works, just as God did from his. Let us, therefore, make every effort to enter that rest, so that no one will perish by following their example of disobedience."*[155] In other words, under the New Covenant, Jesus is our Sabbath, and so to 'keep the Sabbath' is not about striving to avoid what might be construed as work one day a week. It is to keep the faith seven days a week, that Jesus' life and work are enough, and my life is now hidden with His in God (Colossians 3:3).

---

[155] New International Version.

If the life resting in God's work is good in His eyes, what does He think of a life toiling and striving to save itself? The Greek word translated as 'evil' over seventy-five times in the New Testament is '*ponēros*' Listen to Strong's definition of that word: "*full of labours, annoyances, hardships. Pressed and harassed by labours.*"[156] The life toiling to save itself is God's definition of an evil life! But He is not a god who hates a world striving to save itself (John 3:16). He is the Father who so loves this world that He comes out into that world to implore men and women to receive the reconciliation and the life that He freely offers. Just as the father pleaded with the elder brother to stop estranging himself, so we, His Church, in being filled with the Spirit of the Father, are compelled by His love to go out into the world and do the same (Luke 15:28). Note we are not compelled by guilt, but by love (2 Corinthians 5:14, 15).

The apostle Paul calls this the message and the ministry of reconciliation. "*All this is from God, who reconciled us to himself through Christ and gave us the ministry of reconciliation: that God was reconciling the world to himself in Christ, not counting people's sins against them. And he has committed to us the message of reconciliation. We are therefore Christ's ambassadors, as though God were making his appeal through us. We implore you on Christ's behalf: Be reconciled to God. God made him who had no sin to be sin for us, so that in him we might become the righteousness of God.*"[157] (2 Corinthians 5:18-21).

Note the core of this message of reconciliation is not a demand to 'do' but an invitation to 'be': "Be reconciled to God. This is because reconciliation is not a work to be achieved, but a work to be believed! (John 6:28, 29).

Now, to a world determined to save itself and to the church of each generation under the influence of the spirit of that world, the message of the Spirit is still the same. Come! We implore you

---

[156] Strongs Number G4190. https://www.blueletterbible.org/lexicon/g4190/kjv/tr/0-1/

[157] New International Version.

to receive the reconciliation and the joy of the Father over the sufficiency of all His Son has accomplished (Luke 15:6, 9,32). Stop trying to do what Christ has already done. He has reconciled you to Himself. By His grace you can now be who He sees you to be. Be reconciled to God, for your sins are not being counted against you (2 Corinthians 5:19). Can you do that? Can you put your pride in your back pocket and accept righteousness as a gift? Or are you also determined to establish your own righteousness? (Romans 10:1-4). As long as you are, you will insist on mixing a little law into your life with Christ. Every time you do that, you are stepping back from Christ, estranging yourself from participating in the gift of His shared life. You are going back to your old self-life, for only a man who sees himself as having a separate life from God tries to establish his own righteousness. In being married to Nicola, I only have one life, and it is a married life. I don't have a married life and a single life. To live as if I have, would only shrink my married life.

Any gospel that leaves you with the impression that God is looking to you to convince Him that you are worth saving is a shrunken, powerless gospel that can only produce a shrunken, powerless life. Now that's useful if your aim is to control people, for it is always easier to control smaller Christians. Give them a shrunken gospel, and they will never grow out of their fears. They will keep coming to hear what they need to keep doing to keep God content. Listen carefully. If the god you worship is never content, then neither will you ever be! If the god you worship needs you to keep Him content, then you have a very small god!

Being pointed to yourself can never set you free from your self, and Jesus came to set you free from that self, that 'apart from God' life, because, in His words, *"apart from me you can do nothing."*[158] (John 15:5). To try and be someone apart from God is death, as Adam was warned in the garden (Genesis 2:17). Believe the lie that God has withheld his life from you, and you will find yourself in

---

[158] New International Version.

the first Adam, 'dying to become.' Receive the truth that God has not withheld Himself from you, and you will find yourself in the Last Adam 'living to be.' It is by the proclamation of the gospel, the revelation that God has done what we could not—given us life—that men rise from becoming to being, being with God. (Romans 1:16)

The power of grace is that it is precisely not of ourselves, our self-life. As Paul declared to the Ephesians, the life of God is lived by grace through faith, and *"that not of yourselves; it is the gift of God, not of works, lest anyone should boast."*[159] (Ephesians 2:8, 9) Why doesn't God want us to boast? Because only a man who is living a self-made life boasts, and that grieves God because a boasting man is not living in the power of God's grace. A boasting man is living a powerless life.

Let me give you another description of boasting. It is when believers start judging the world as less worthy in God's eyes, because we have either forgotten or never saw clearly that all we have received from God came as the gift of His grace. As Paul said to the Corinthians, *"What do you have that you did not receive? And if you did receive it, why do you boast as if you did not?"*[160] (1 Corinthians 4:7) The Gospel is the most powerful message in the world, but that power is all of God, not of man. That power is grace, not self-effort, and so whenever in history a little law has been added to the gospel of grace, power has been stripped from the gospel, and a shrunken gospel has only ever borne shrunken believers. How can I convince you that's not the gospel? I don't have to. I only ask you to look into your own heart. If today you cannot find there a joy inexpressible and full of glory, then ask the Holy Spirit to show you why. Ask Him to show you why feet that were made to run into the streets with good news, can now only walk to church for more good advice.

How are a people who have lived all their lives in darkness, to perceive what darkness is? Which is a more effective way to

---

[159] New King James Version.
[160] New International Version.

persuade them: to preach about the dangers of darkness, or to show them light? The most effective way to awaken a nation to the reality of the darkness of lives separated from God, is to present them with the shining reality of lives lived in communion with God (Matthew 5:14-16). If the gospel we have been raised under has left us still thinking of ourselves (and so living) as mere men (1 Corinthians 3:3, Colossians 2:20), then we may have been raised under it, but we have not been raised by it! The gospel that the apostle Paul preached lifted men's thinking and so their living into the heavenly realm, for it is only in living from there that the Church can reveal the heavenly man, the new creation: Christ in His body (Colossians 3:1-4).

In our rush to achieve, we fail to receive. In our rush to achieve for Him, so often we have neglected to appreciate just what a great and glorious salvation we have received from Him. All that we already have in Christ is far beyond what our earthly imagination or experience has yet revealed (1 Corinthians 2:9, 10). This revelation of the unbounded generosity of the Father, to have blessed us in Christ with every spiritual blessing (Ephesians 1:3), leads our souls into such a profound rest, that our heart motives in life and ministry are formed and informed not by a fear of failure, but by pure thanksgiving. This thanksgiving is the life He always purposed for us (1 Thessalonians 5:16-18). Surely also, this is the most powerful spiritual warfare that the Church can engage in: to participate in the victory celebrations of heaven, by trumpeting the finished work of Christ as sufficient to bring life and immortality to all who will receive Him (Ephesians 2:8, 9). This is the dawn that death flees from, the glory of the Lord rising on us, His eternal life rising in us.

What brings this 'to light' in the darkness of this world, is the proclamation of the gospel of Christ and Him crucified (2 Timothy 1:10). Only the undiluted message of a victory won and eternal life freely gifted and waiting to be received, can match the description the angels gave at Christ's birth: *"good tidings of great joy, which will be to all people"*[161] (Luke 2:10). Only such a gospel can be worthy of the magnitude of the invitation of the Father, *"But we had to celebrate and rejoice, because this brother of yours was dead and has begun to live, and was lost and has been found."*[162] (Luke 15:32). To receive the gospel in truth, is to allow ourselves to be led into a house of music and dancing, the heart of the Father over His children (Luke 15:25). The gospel we preach must carry the sound of this celebration, the sound of confidence in Christ's work, a sound that a generation of souls has searched for in vain among the cacophony of self-help and self-effort gospels of this world. (Colossians 2:20).

At this hour in history, the world is again setting its hope on what man can do to save humanity. So, what better hour for the Church to return to the only truth that sets men free from themselves: the declaration that what Christ has done is sufficient for all the needs of all men (2 Corinthians 5:19). Here is the message that still sounds like foolishness to the world: it is finished! All that needs to be done, has been done through Christ. (John 19:30).

How much faith does God have in His Word? Enough to see you as whom He declares you to be, not whom your earthly record declares you to be. He is the God who can see past your past. The Holy Spirit is the spirit of faith that empowers our hearts to perceive the highest calling of God on our lives: our sonship in Christ that transcends our earthly record (2 Timothy 1:9). By this empowerment, His Church rises. No longer shackled to our past life, we can grow up into His present life, and through such a rising in His Church, His glory dawns on the earth (Isaiah 60:1-3). As the old hymn says, *'the things of this world grow strangely dim in the light of His glory and grace.'*[163] In the light of the resurrected Christ, we can see that one of the things of this world is death. As the gospel dawns as news (not instruction), the Spirit illuminates our lives with

---

[161] New King James Version.
[162] New American Standard Bible.
[163] "Turn your eyes upon Jesus" Helen Howarth Lemmel.

the presence of God, and before such a dawn, death grows strangely dim. When the Gospel is heard as news of a finished work, death pales at that news!

If Paul and Silas had only seen as the world sees, then while lying in that jail in Philippi they would have seen themselves as 'forsaken by God.' But in the darkness of that cell, they found themselves seeing more clearly than ever, seeing by the Spirit. That night a different sound was heard in that jail, not the cries of men forsaken by God, but the song of men hidden in God. (Acts 16:25). It was a song that so resonated with a creation groaning for men to see and speak as sons of God, that the very stones around them cried out and gave up their prisoners (Acts 16:26, Romans 8:19-22). When the jailer called for light to see by, he found in their cell a light already shining!

Paul and Silas did not sing in the hope that if they sang well enough or long enough, God might answer. They sang as men who carried God's answer, Christ, and were joyfully carrying that answer into the darkest places on earth. Their lives were a light shining in the darkness because they lived not waiting for a better day but living in the eternal day of the Lord. They were the light of Christ dawning on those sitting in great darkness. They were not proclaiming a message of what might be, but of what is. In knowing that reality, they were not waiting for freedom; they were living in a freedom that chains or walls could not contain (2 Cor. 3:17). So captivated were the other prisoners, that when the doors flew open, they didn't move. They could not bring themselves to run back out into a world where they had never found such liberty (Acts 16:28). Once men see the liberty the Spirit brings, the pale imitations this world offers lose their power (Galatians 5:16).

Selah! Let the Church hear the song of heaven: thanksgiving for what is! Let the sound of that song begin to rise over a generation who have sat in darkness. Let our song not be about a better day to come, for only the dawn dispels the darkness, not the promise of the dawn. Let us not despair at the darkness around us, for this is very day for which we were called. For what better place for the children of light, the children of what is, to shine, than a world darkened by the fear of what might be! (Philippians 2:15).

To see the Kingdom come on earth as it is in heaven, we must preach the Gospel on earth as it is in heaven. In heaven it is not good advice on what might be, but the good news of what is! To a world blinded and deafened by the age of information, let us proclaim what can only be seen by the Spirit, for still today at the sound of such a song, the greatest prison in the world opens, the unbelieving heart.

Epilogue

When our son Christopher was three years of age, one of my sisters came to visit us. She had been looking forward to talking to him and wanted to find out what his level of understanding was. She sat him down and proceeded to ask a series of questions, such as 'What age are you? What is your favourite food?' Each simple question elicited an equally simple response, usually a one-word answer. Eventually my sister declared, "Isn't this great Christopher, we are having a conversation." We have never forgotten the answer that little boy gave her. He looked straight at her and said, "You are asking me questions and I am giving you the answers, but that's not a conversation!"

Now that you have read this book, you too may have a few questions. I would encourage you to bring them to the one who already knows your questions and why you carry them. He is not afraid of difficult questions, for He knows that they are an essential aspect of growing up. We are more likely to fall into error without them, and as the apostle Peter said, the best way to avoid falling into error, is to grow in the grace and knowledge of Him who is the answer to all our questions. (2Peter3:18)

Down through the ages of the Church, there have always been questions that have arisen in society that have divided the opinions of believers and caused controversy in the body of Christ. Often as a minister, I have had sincere believers come to me and say, "Tell me what you think. Is it right for a Christian to … ?" Now when it comes to answering such questions, I have found it helpful to simply remember that my calling is primarily in the field of good news, not good advice. My role is not to tell people what to think, but to give them the truth that teaches them how to think.

The Gospel is the truth that enables people to think from thanksgiving, not from fear, and I have found that decisions made from thanksgiving always bear better fruit than those made from fear (1Thessalonians 5:18). In this digital age, we are the generation of the Church that has more access to information than any before us. But no matter what the issue is, from vaccines to artificial intelligence, information without love cannot bring us to Christlikeness, and any decision founded on fear will never bear the fruit of a decision founded on thanksgiving.

Today, social media has increasingly become the public forum where people accuse each other before the world. But what's the point of seeking to be 'right' on an issue, when our attitude to those who oppose our position remains full of fear, not love? What's the point of being right, when the way we are being 'right' is pushing others away from Christ? Listen again to what the apostle Paul told the Corinthians, who were so set on being proved right that they were taking each other to court in front of the world: *"Actually, then, it is already a defeat for you, that you have lawsuits with one another. Why not rather suffer the wrong? Why not rather be defrauded?"*[164] (1 Corinthians 6:7).

Without love, it is possible to hold all the right positions on all the right moral issues of the day, only to end up as far from the heart of God as the elder brother lecturing his own father on the rights and wrongs of welcoming home the prodigal. What's the point of wanting to be seen to be right, when the heart of Christ (felt by Paul for his Jewish brothers) was rather to be wrong and cursed and cut off from God, than for them to perish? (Romans 9:3). As nations, communities, and families divide today over who is right, our world's greatest need remains to know the heart of Him who

---

[164] New American Standard Version.

went to the Cross, not so that He would be right but so that we who were his enemies could be right. To be filled with the Spirit of Him who is Love, is not to ask, "What should I do in order that I be right?" but rather, "What should I do in order that my brother be right?" for a self-centred life can never be right in the eyes of God.

At the beginning of Chapter eight of his first letter to the Corinthians, Paul writes on one such question of what is right for a Christian. He begins *"Now about food sacrificed to idols:"*[165] There follows not a simple yes or no, but rather three chapters explaining why his answer can't be as simple as yes or no, because for Paul the fundamental question was not whether his action made him right or wrong, but rather what effect it would have on others! (1 Corinthians 10:31-33). The Church has always grown up in Christ, not through the impartation of knowledge alone, but through the impartation of love (Ephesians 4:15, 16). To be filled with the Spirit, is to be filled with the love of God and thus a thanksgiving that lifts your eyes off yourself (Romans 5:5). That's why the best answer to a generation dividing again and again over all the questions before us, is simply to keep preaching the Gospel. It is the only news that fills men with the love that casts out fear, even the fear of not being right. That's because only the Gospel can reveal us to be right in God's sight, not because we did the right thing but because He did! Only the gospel reveals us to be now right, because we are now right where He wanted us to be: hidden with Christ in God (Colossians 3:1-4). Nothing you or I will ever do will make us more right than that!

So, what is the right thing to do? Stop trying to make yourself right. Accept that was Christ's work, and He has done it so well that you and I are now free to reckon ourselves dead and do the right thing for the world that He gave Himself for. Stop trying to save yourself. Look up and see that in Christ, the Father who never left us to save ourselves walked through the chaos and took hold of your life. In love He embraced you, for Heaven couldn't wait!

---

[165] New International Version.

www.ingramcontent.com/pod-product-compliance
Ingram Content Group UK Ltd.
Pitfield, Milton Keynes, MK11 3LW, UK
UKHW041445070126
466727UK00001B/41